Humanizing the Classroom

Humanizing the Classroom

Using Role-Plays to Teach Social and Emotional Skills in Middle School and High School

Kristin Stuart Valdes

ROWMAN & LITTLEFIELD
Lanham • Boulder • New York • London

Published by Rowman & Littlefield
An imprint of The Rowman & Littlefield Publishing Group, Inc.
4501 Forbes Boulevard, Suite 200, Lanham, Maryland 20706
www.rowman.com

6 Tinworth Street, London SE11 5AL

British Library Cataloguing in Publication Information Available

Library of Congress Cataloging-in-Publication Data

Names: Valdes, Kristin Stuart, 1967– author.
Title: Humanizing the classroom : using role-plays to teach social and emotional skills in middle school and high school / Kristin Stuart Valdes.
Description: Lanham, Maryland : Rowman & Littlefield, [2019] | Includes bibliographical references.
Identifiers: LCCN 2018059658 (print) | LCCN 2019007541 (ebook) | ISBN 9781475840483 (Electronic) | ISBN 9781475840469 (cloth : alk. paper) | ISBN 9781475840476 (pbk. : alk. paper)
Subjects: LCSH: Affective education. | Emotional intelligence—Study and teaching (Middle school) | Emotional intelligence—Study and teaching (Secondary) | Social learning. | Role playing.
Classification: LCC LB1072 (ebook) | LCC LB1072 .V35 2019 (print) | DDC 370.15/34—dc23
LC record available at https://lccn.loc.gov/2018059658

Printed in the United States of America

This book is dedicated to all the public school students in the gorgeously diverse five boroughs of New York City. You all navigate the complex world in which you live with more grace and courage than many of the adults with whom you share it. My eighteen years of work with you has been a human gift beyond measure. Like the gift of love or the gift of kindness, it has opened my mind and heart in ways that go beyond the content of any curriculum. I look forward to being a citizen in the world that you will help create.

Contents

I: Foundations   **1**

1   Why and How Should We Teach Social and Emotional Skills?   3

2   Social and Emotional Learning Role-Plays   15

3   Facilitating Collaborative, Creative, and Experiential Learning   35

4   Social and Emotional Learning and Culturally Responsive Teaching   53

II: SEL Role-Plays for the Classroom   **63**

5   Curriculum Organization   65

6   The Lessons   75

References   165

About the Author   167

I

Foundations

ONE

Why and How Should We Teach
Social and Emotional Skills?

WHY TEACH SOCIAL AND EMOTIONAL SKILLS?

Many educators believe that students need more social and emotional skills, but there is not a consensus about whether educators should be the ones to impart them. Some educators see themselves as content area specialists and believe that the classroom is strictly for academic learning, while others believe in educating the whole child, but are unsure about the pedagogical methods for doing so.

Whether you believe that schools should take on the task of teaching social and emotional skills, or whether you believe that this is an issue for parents or counselors, is a complex and personal decision. But, if you believe that students need these skills, there are a wealth of social and emotional learning programs that can provide curricular material. This book could be counted as one such source.

The concept that we should become educated about our own emotional lives can be traced to some of the earliest theories of education. The ancient aphorism "know thyself" inscribed on the Temple of Delphi was paving the way for what we may now refer to as social and emotional learning (SEL). SEL is an umbrella term that refers to any program that has as its philosophical underpinning the belief that students can be taught skills to help them manage their own emotions and conflicts. The term was first coined by Peter Salovey, professor and psychologist at Yale University, and John Mayer, professor and psychologist at the University of New Hampshire, but was popularized by Daniel Goleman in his watershed book *Emotional Intelligence*.

Since the publication of *Emotional Intelligence*, many social and emotional learning programs have emerged for use in our schools. Peer mediation programs, restorative justice programs, mindfulness programs, peer-to-peer counseling programs, positive behavior management programs, growth mindset programs, and social and emotional learning skill-based curricula could all fall under the social and emotional learning umbrella.

In general, these programs propose that students can be taught skills to better manage their own emotions, behaviors, and conflicts, and by learning these skills students will perform better academically, have fewer disciplinary issues, and gain greater autonomy. And, research has shown that autonomy is one of humankind's most powerful sources for internal motivation. Hence, many students truly take to the learning experiences in these programs as they sense the benefits that the experiences will have on their own lives and relationships, both in and out of school.

However, the idea that students will change their own behavior for the betterment of themselves and their community can be a difficult concept for adults to accept. Many educators consciously or unconsciously categorize students into two categories: "good" and "bad." Many of these categorizations are formed by conscious or unconscious biases based on class, ethnicity, language of origin, social groupings, family reputation, and/or behavior outside of school.

Once we have formed biases about a student, it can be hard to imagine that a social and emotional learning program would help them "change." Our biases often become our fixed attitudes, opinions, and convictions. In addition, if we hold such biases, we may also believe that social and emotional learning programs are for students whose behavior we perceive to be problematic, when in actuality social and emotional learning programs provide skill-building opportunities for *all* members of the school community—students and adults alike. Social and emotional learning programs are largely primary preventative programs wherein social and emotional skills are taught to all students, not a select few who have been labelled as problematic.

By teaching these skills regularly, to everyone in the school community, schools build a community that possesses a broad base of social and emotional skills that can be drawn on in moments of crisis. This organic spreading and sharing of skills often changes approaches to discipline. As students gain skills to help themselves in moments of crisis, and peers become more adept at supporting one another, the often unconscious bias that adults develop about "difficult" students may begin to shift, as may the school's approach to discipline.

Through regularly teaching social and emotional skills to their students, adults often realize that it is not only the students that need to work on developing self-awareness, self-management, social awareness, relationship building, and responsible decision-making capacities. If we are honest with ourselves, most of us will acknowledge that we also need to develop more skills in these areas.

If we actively involve ourselves in teaching social and emotional learning skills, we will quickly realize that we are engaged in a parallel process, whereby we are learning the very skills that we are teaching, often as we are teaching them—for there are no content area "experts" in social and emotional learning. We are all students on the same journey. While we may be at different places on the path, every new life experience or interaction presents new opportunities about how to manage ourselves, our communication, our inner emotional life, and our moments of conflict.

RESISTANCE TO SEL

One of the great fears educators hold about social and emotional learning programs is that such programs will take the place of consequences for unwanted behavior. At the core of these fears is an idea that supporting students' autonomous learning about themselves and their own feelings and experiences will undermine the authority that adults hold in the disciplinary process. In other words, if a child displays unwanted behavior, many adults feel that student must accept their punishment and that part of their punishment is being stripped of their voice.

But, teaching children skills to resolve their own problems does not mean that they do not receive consequences for challenging behavior. It means that in conjunction with whatever disciplinary action is taken, adults will engage the student in social and emotional skill building, which will help them deal with the emotions that caused the unwanted behavior. This engagement with the student will help them to manage their emotions in a more positive way the next time they are triggered by a similar situation.

For example, a student who is removed from class or school for physically fighting can still be taught about anger triggers, cooling down strategies, and ways to respect various points of view. And, if this student is taught such skills, and allowed to practice them in a supportive and no-fault zone, they will be less likely to physically fight in the future.

In conclusion, many people believe that students need social and emotional skills, but there is some difference of opinion about how these skills should be taught. There is also a fear among educators, who in theory support the teaching of social and emotional skills, about how social and emotional initiatives will interact with discipline policies.

Differences of opinion and skepticism are healthy responses to new or unfamiliar ideas. It is our differences of opinion that allow us to create rich and complex dialogues. It is our skepticism that drives us to seek evidence, both for a new idea and against it, as we actively imagine the reality of new and unfamiliar ideas in action.

For many educators social and emotional learning initiatives are a relatively new concept. Using role-plays to teach social and emotional skills for K-12 students, as this book proposes, may bring up strong opinions and skepticism, but it may also give rise to new and exciting ideas for your classroom. I invite you to bring your questions, your skepticism, and your own creative ideas to your reading of this book, to take from it what you find interesting, and to shape the material in your classroom and with your students in a way that suits both you and them.

THE CASE FOR A SOCIAL AND EMOTIONAL LEARNING PEDAGOGY

The Collaborative for Academic, Social, and Emotional Learning has defined five competencies for social and emotional learning:

1. Self-Awareness
2. Self-Management
3. Social Awareness
4. Relationship Skills
5. Responsible Decision-Making

These competencies are very useful for conceptualizing the scope of social and emotional learning as a whole. Underneath each of these competencies there are a variety of skills that can be taught to help adults and children alike. Skills such as articulating feelings; reading body language; cooling down techniques; self-talk and mindfulness; deep listening; practicing empathy; assertive communication; developing neutrality; embracing contrasting points of view; recognizing and countering bias, prejudice, and discrimination; and de-escalating conflict would all support the development of these overarching competencies. As mentioned earlier, many programs provide rich curricular material for teaching these skills, and others.

But, what is often ignored in social and emotional learning curricula is the question of pedagogy, or the methods by which we should teach social and emotional learning skills. Social and emotional learning engages adults and students in a way that most academic subject areas do not. By asking us to reflect upon our own inner emotional lives, our own personal choices, and our own relationships in light of new skills that will offer us other choices, social and emotional learning asks us to search for subjective applications for objective material.

This is very different than asking students to intellectually understand information and repeat it (as on a history test) or intellectually understand and apply it (as in a math problem or science experiment). The "learning" in social and emotional learning is a different kind of learning. It requires us to engage our minds, our hearts, and our bodies in a self-reflective process of inquiry that is ultimately about better understanding ourselves and how we move through the world in which we live.

For this reason, there will always be multiple "right answers" in social and emotional learning lessons. Each student is the master of their own learning because each individual student has the ultimate knowledge of their own life, their own personal environment, and their own struggles. Each student is their own best teacher because it will be up to each student to determine how to best apply social and emotional learning skills and concepts in their own lives. Each student is the best assessor of their own social and emotional learning and development because only the individual themselves can apply social and emotional learning concepts in their own lives, experience the success or failure of that application, and decide what refinements to make in the future.

This is very different than much academic assessment, which allows for one "right" answer, or even academic discussions, which teachers consciously or unconsciously steer in the direction they feel is "right." Assessment of academic learning is often done by someone besides the student themselves. And, this assessment is most often reached by observing a student's ability to perform and demonstrate knowledge within an academic environment. Social and emotional learning gives students skills and concepts within an academic environment, but the only way they can be truly learned and assessed is by applying them in life.

In short, social and emotional learning content engages us in a way that most academic subjects do not. Social and emotional learning asks us to learn by applying skills and concepts individually and uniquely in the real living of our own lives. It asks us to do this repeatedly as a practice, to continually reflect upon our practice, and to change our behavior as a result of what we learn.

Because this entire process is so different than academic learning, we need to think more deeply about aligning our pedagogy with our content because teaching a lesson on self-talk, for example, is very different than teaching a lesson on long form multiplication. So, how do we best teach social and emotional learning skills, and what pedagogy best supports learning in this complex content area that challenges each individual student to be their own best teacher?

SOCIAL EMOTIONAL LEARNING IS LIMBIC SYSTEM LEARNING

In order to teach social and emotional learning effectively, we need an approach that meets the challenges of social and emotional learning content. We need an approach that allows us to safely share personal information without feeling overwhelmed by vulnerability. We need an approach that provides an objective framework for the learning moments embedded in our personal experiences. And, we need an approach that gives us a chance to practice new social and emotional learning skills *before* attempting to put them into practice in our real lives. Role-plays, which combine limbic system learning and experiential learning, are an exciting solution to the pedagogical challenges of teaching social and emotional learning effectively.

From a neuroscience perspective, social and emotional learning can be understood to take place in the brain's limbic system. The limbic system governs emotions, impulses, habitual reactions, perceptions of spatial relationships, and long-term memory. It is a very different brain center than the vast neocortex, which, among other things, governs language acquisition and analytical ability. And, because it governs the processing of different content, it learns differently. Daniel Goleman's research suggests that the limbic system learns best with practice, one-on-one feedback, and positive motivation.

Learning new behaviors, which is the goal of all social and emotional learning programs, is hard work. Anyone who has repeatedly been asked to remember to close the bathroom door or take out the trash can attest to this. It involves understanding your habitual responses and why you have them, learning new behaviors, practicing these new behaviors or responses, and repeating them until new behaviors become new habits. In order to successfully change our behaviors around how we deal with our emotions, which is even more difficult than physical tasks like remembering to close a door, we need to engage our limbic system.

Therefore, from a neuroscience perspective, the successful acquisition of new social and emotional learning skills over time has more in common with learning how to play the piano, learning how to do a pirouette, or learning how to shoot a free throw in basketball than it does with learning how to add or subtract. For, in each of these examples, a student would be encouraged to physically practice the task multiple times, the student would be provided with feedback on the practice itself (not simply the end result), and the student would be motivated by their own interest.

Just as Goleman's research suggests, and as other limbic system learners like musicians, artists, dancers, and athletes can attest, we need to engage in skills practice, we need to receive feedback on our practice itself, and we need to connect with our personal motivations for engaging in a process of growth and change. However, many well-written social and emotional learning curricula ignore the basics of limbic system learning.

Some programs take an academic approach that emphasizes passive learning, memorization, and academic skill practice. For example, a character education program might identify a value of the month such as "honesty" and run an essay contest for student writing on that subject.

The winner of such a contest would be chosen because of the academic skills associated with their writing rather than the author's ability to practice the self-awareness, self-management, and relationship-building skills that are required to actually *be* honest in daily life and in difficult situations.

Some programs associate social and emotional learning with behavior management and may have a punitive approach to teaching social and emotional skills. For example, a school climate program might suggest community service projects for kids who have misbehaved. But, this communicates that community service is a punitive intervention to a crisis rather than part of building our social awareness skills on a regular basis.

Lastly, some programs associate social and emotional learning with psychology and thus employ a therapeutic model, which implies private, one-on-one sessions. For instance, a guidance counselor may work on building trust with an individual student who shares their narrative account of a recent fight. But that same counselor may not have the time or resources to allow for skills practice around identifying anger triggers and cooling down strategies in a group context where these fights often happen.

When our pedagogical approaches to social and emotional learning ignore the basics of limbic system learning—practice, one-on-one feedback on that practice, and positive motivation—we are often underwhelmed with the results. We may find that the student who won the essay contest on honesty is involved in spreading gossip, or that the students who did community service for fighting continue their feud when their service is complete, or that the student who shared his individual story with the counselor returns to class and continues to be disruptive. We may be confused and frustrated with the ineffectiveness of our efforts and even decide that social and emotional learning "doesn't work" without realizing that our pedagogy did not meet the challenges of our content.

But, would we ever expect a musician, artist, or athlete to improve without practice? Many an aspiring musician is discouraged by the fact that understanding music theory does not mean that one can play an instrument. Many an aspirating artist is frustrated by the realization that understanding color theory will not translate directly into one's ability to paint well. And, many an aspiring athlete is frustrated by the fact that being able to explain a play will not translate into one's ability to execute it.

The arts and athletics provide a powerful example of the difference in neocortical or academic learning and limbic system learning because they ultimately demand that practitioners change their behavior in order to improve. In social and emotional learning, our goal of changing behavior, albeit for different reasons, is the same.

Most people associate role-plays with drama or theater class. But, upon a closer look, role-plays, by their very nature, are structured to incorporate the practice, one-on-one feedback on that practice, and positive motivation that is so important in limbic system learning. From a neuroscience perspective, role-plays are an excellent way to "wake up" limbic system learning. So, they are an excellent place to start in our search for a pedagogy that supports social and emotional learning skill acquisition. But, how can we make the most of role-plays, from a pedagogical standpoint? To answer this, we need to ask ourselves what kind of practice is the most powerful.

A NOTE ON PRACTICE

Practice could be defined as the repeated performance of a distinct skill, which, once mastered, can be used as the basis of support for the acquisition of more complex skills. Theater, the visual arts, music, and sports all bring to mind hours of repetitive practice time aimed at improving performance. But, there are many different kinds of practice and some are more effective than others.

In his book *PEAK: Secrets from the New Science of Expertise*, psychologist Anders Ericsson (with coauthor Robert Poole) defines three distinct types of practice. *Naive practice* is something that many of us experience when we take up a hobby. We learn about what we want to do, be it play tennis or play chess; we practice the fundamental skills to the point that we are competent enough to enjoy the activity; and then we stop practice and rest in our comfort zone. *Purposeful practice* involves a concerted effort to improve a specific skill by clearly defining a goal, getting some feedback from others, and stepping out of our comfort zone, occasionally, to improve our performance. *Deliberate practice* builds on purposeful practice by eliciting the feedback of an expert, consistently stepping out of our comfort zone, and using deep concentration to build upon our existing skill set.

Ericsson is the originator of the oft-quoted "10,000 hours rule" for developing expertise through practice. In response to the popular use of his research, he has also talked about needing to take into account the type of practice that one does when referring to the "10,000 hour rule." Someone who is involved in naive practice may well put in 10,000 hours of practice time but never reach any level of expertise. However, someone who practices deliberately may reach a recognizable level of expertise before 10,000 hours of practice.

In the classroom, where we are teaching social and emotional learning skills, deliberate practice would involve a teacher deeply connected to the content, who is willing to push the students out of their comfort zones as they explore it, and would allow for repeated practice to refine social and emotional skills. Traditional or passive instruction will not be effective in helping students internalize social and emotional skills nor will it build the confidence needed to apply the skills in their own lives. Teachers will have to engage in complex and creative facilitation in order to support this type of learning and engagement. But, we will get to that later.

In conclusion, like the arts and sports, social and emotional learning is limbic system learning. It is embodied learning. If we can "wake up" the limbic system with deliberate practice, where teacher-facilitators push students out of their comfort zones as they practice new skills, then social and emotional learning will have a greater chance of taking root in the hearts, minds, and bodies of our students and result in behavioral changes in their lives.

AS CLOSE AS WE CAN GET: EXPERIENTIAL LEARNING MODELS AND ROLE-PLAYS

While we understand that limbic system learning requires practice and that deliberate practice with a teacher-facilitator who is willing to push students out of their comfort zone is optimal, what actual teaching method shall we draw from? When we consider that social and emotional learning teaches various life skills and that role-plays can be used to explore real-life experiences, experiential learning pedagogy presents a powerful option.

The general concept of learning through experience goes back to 350 BC, when Aristotle wrote, "For the things we have to learn before we can do them, we learn *by* doing them" (emphasis mine). But, in the 1970s, David A. Kolb helped to develop a modern theory of experiential learning, or learning by doing. His pragmatic approach offers four simple stages associated with experiential learning:

1. Concrete experience
2. Reflective observation
3. Abstract conceptualization
4. Active experimentation

We all have gone through the four stages of experiential learning throughout our own lives, in and out of the classroom. Anyone who has learned how to ride a bike first looked at the bike, held it, felt its weight, and hopped on to give it a try (concrete experience). After toppling down to the ground, most of us got up and tried to figure out why we fell (reflective observation). We then strategized, hopefully with the help of someone older and wiser, about what we should do differently on our second attempt (abstract conceptualization). And, finally, we applied these ideas in our second, third, and fourth attempts at maintaining our balance (active experimentation).

These stages can be used as a pedagogical approach for any experiential learning lessons in any subject area. For example, it's easy to imagine how sampling beach grasses over a span of two years would deepen student understanding of soil erosion. It's clear that participating in school board elections would give students a deep appreciation for the complexities of democracy. And, we can imagine how handling museum artifacts would give students a more nuanced understanding of living in a time before automation. Experiential learning deepens understanding and gives students confidence with subject matter that is based in their own, unique experiences. Research has shown that experiential learning increases academic performance.

Like the other arts, role-plays are inherently and by nature experiential, meaning they engage the five senses. While music explores the auditory sense, dance explores the kinetic sense, and the fine arts explore visual and tactile senses, role-plays, being a close approximation of real life, explore the integration of all the senses. By involving the five senses and the emotions of learners, experiential learning increases not only their engagement with the material, but also their memory and their ability to understand the nuances of complex subject matter. We want the same to happen with social and emotional skills and learning, and role-plays can help.

The skills we want to teach in social and emotional learning arise from real-life issues and challenges. But, we wouldn't want to incite an actual fight in order to teach about cooling down strategies. We wouldn't want to actually bully someone in order to teach about assertiveness skills. And, we wouldn't want to actively isolate a student in order to teach empathy. In short, we wouldn't want to incite a real situation where social and emotional skills could be practiced because this would create confusion, division, and deep harm. Throwing a non-swimmer off of the high diving board into the deep end of the pool will not teach them to swim. In fact, they could drown.

Role-plays provide a very close approximation of the real-life experiences of difficult emotions and conflict while, at the same time, providing a safe distance from the actual experiences themselves. They are an excellent way to provide appropriate scaffolding for learning social and emotional skills. They can be thought of as a form of experiential learning that actively engages the limbic system in safe and deliberate practice in order that students may acquire new social and emotional skills to use in their own lives.

In conclusion, the Collaborative for Academic, Social, and Emotional Learning has identified five competencies for social and emotional learning: self-awareness, self-management, social awareness, relationship skills, and responsible decision-making. Many curricula provide lessons for teaching skills that would fall under these competency headings, but the question of social and emotional learning pedagogy is often ignored.

Unlike many other social and emotional learning curriculum, this book provides both a pedagogical model and curricular material for teaching social and emotional skills. The pedagogical model is explored in detail and includes best practices for role-plays as well as facilitation techniques. These techniques include an exploration of culturally responsive practices and how they are essential to teaching social and emotional learning effectively. Lastly, the curriculum is organized in multiple, flexible tracks that allow for student and teacher interest to drive the progress of learning.

From Daniel Goleman's research we know that social and emotional learning takes place in the limbic system, which governs emotions and habitual responses. The limbic system requires practice, one-on-one feedback, and positive motivation in order for new behaviors to take hold.

From Anders Ericsson's work on practice, we know that deliberate practice, where an engaged observer pushes us to move out of our comfort zone, is the most effective type of practice. We would want to prepare teachers to support their students in deliberate practice of new social and emotional skills, as this will lead to the deepest level of learning and skill acquisition.

And, from the work of David A. Kolb, we can see that an experiential learning process applied to the use of role-plays can create a safe space for students to build social and emotional skills. Ultimately, these skills will be tested in their real lives. But, if we provide a safe space for students to engage in a concrete experience, reflective observation, abstract conceptualization, and active experimentation, and if they are encouraged to deliberately practice the social and emotional skills they learn in this process, they will have more success in their attempts at changing their behavior in their own lives.

TWO

Social and Emotional Learning Role-Plays

For many of us, our first association of role-plays is with drama or theater class. We assume there is a script that has already been written, and a teacher who prepares student actors to embody the characters for a performance in front of an audience. The audience will arrive for the performance ready to be entertained in some way, and out of respect for the actors, they won't talk during the performance or engage them in direct dialogue. They will sit passively during the entire performance, and will likely clap to show their appreciation at the conclusion, whether or not the goal of being entertained was actually reached.

But, an effective classroom role-play is different from "putting on a show." First, the student actors do not use prewritten scripts. Actors in classroom role-plays improvise their lines based on a common understanding of the issue that will be explored in the role-play.

Second, the audience does not sit passively for the duration of a performance. Instead, the actors and audience members collaborate in a creative dialogue exploring the issue, the various plots twists that the story could take, the many ways the characters could address the problem that arises in the story, what can be learned about the effectiveness of the social-emotional skills employed by the characters, and how the audience members may use these skills in their own lives. Audience members may even change roles and participate as actors themselves.

Lastly, because the actors and audience are engaged in a creative and collaborative dialogue throughout a classroom role-play, the nature of the teacher's job shifts. Rather than the traditional role that drama teachers play—helping actors memorize lines and develop their characters, blocking their movements on stage, and otherwise directing a "production" with all that entails—the teachers of classroom role-plays function

15

as teacher-facilitators of student dialogue. As the dialogue in classroom role-plays is complex, teachers will need to develop complex facilitation skills in order to support it.

Classroom role-plays are a form of experiential learning that incorporates kinetic, auditory, and visual modalities to convey content and information. Research tells us that when modalities are incorporated into the teaching of academic subjects, more students can engage in the content that is being shared. For instance, if a kinetic learner is struggling with multiplication and they are allowed to physically count the floor tiles in an area of the room measuring three tiles horizontally and four tiles vertically, they may be able to return from this exercise with a deeper understanding of the equation "$3 \times 4 = 12$." Modal learning approaches help students process new information, deepen their understanding, and synthesize complex ideas quickly.

One could argue that all experiential learning is modal learning, and this may be true. But, not all modal learning is experiential, as in the above example of a kinetic approach to learning multiplication. Not every incorporation of learning styles in the delivery of content is done through Kolb's classic experiential learning framework of experience, observation/reflection, conceptualization, and experimentation.

But, classroom role-plays are both experiential and modal. They provide all class members with direct experience of an issue or conflict and the chance to practice various responses to that conflict in the experience, observation/reflection, conceptualization, and experimentation framework. And, they provide additional information about that issue or conflict that students may glean through the visual, auditory, and kinetic modalities utilized in the role-play.

So, for a student who has trouble following the dialogue in a role-play, they can use the tone of the actor's voice to get contextual clues about its meaning. For students who are not sure of the power dynamics in the issue being explored, they can look to the physical interplay of the actors for more information. For students who struggle to synthesize larger themes, they can draw on all the modalities encompassed by the role-play to gather more information. For example, in response to a synthesis question such as, "Which character has the most to lose in this conflict and why?" a student might visually recall how a character was standing to get clues to their deeper feelings, or compare the tone of voice of the various characters to interpret who dominated the conversation.

Both the experiential nature of role-plays and the fact that they employ the visual, auditory, and kinetic modalities allows students to develop a deeper understanding of the issues being explored. The more deeply students understand the issues, the greater chance there is that they will use the social and emotional skills they learn in their real lives. So, how can we set up role-plays to best exploit all the rich learning opportunities embedded within them?

SETTING THE STAGE

In classroom role-plays, we obviously will not have the proscenium stage that is found in so many school auditoriums. Nor will we be expecting the audience to sit in passive silence. So we must set up the room so that there is a space for freedom of movement for the student actors, good sight lines for the audience as they observe the action of the role-play, and good sight lines for the actors, audience, and teacher-facilitator as the group engages in reflection, discussion, and creative collaboration.

A traditional classroom setup of desks in rows is not optimal. The space at the front of the room is often quite narrow and is intended to allow for the movement of one person: a teacher. In addition, sight lines for peer-to-peer discussion are compromised as students are meant to see the teacher and the teacher alone, but in classroom role-plays we want to encourage students to engage in peer-to-peer dialogue. If your classroom is currently set up this way, it will be important to make the effort to move the desks into another format to allow for the deepest learning to take place.

One suggestion is moving the desks to the outer perimeter of the room and arranging the chairs in a circle in the center. This creates good sight lines for everyone in the class because in a circle everyone can see everyone else's eyes, which is important for peer-to-peer discussions. A circle also provides an open space in the center where the role-play can take place. Finally, since everyone has an equally good view of the center of the circle, no one is blocked from viewing the action of the role-play.

A horseshoe arrangement of desks or chairs can also work well. Like a circle, it also allows for good sight lines and an open space for the role-play to take place. In addition, a horseshoe creates a sort of proscenium, which can help define the area for action, allows actors to enter and exit the action, and affords the teacher-facilitator a strong position from which to facilitate peer-to-peer dialogue.

Although it may seem inconvenient to rearrange your room for a classroom role-play, it is worth the effort. There needs to be ample space for physical movement in order to take advantage of the full experiential and modal learning opportunities embedded within them. In addition, you and your students will be more able to easily engage in reflection, discussion, and creative collaboration.

ENGAGING KINETIC AWARENESS

In every class there will be students who gravitate toward acting or performing and those who shy away from it. In a traditional drama class, we might choose our "stars" based on their natural placement on the introvert/extrovert continuum.

But a classroom role-play is not a traditional performance or show, and we are not looking for stars but for participants. A classroom role-play is a modal learning experience that increases creative collaboration and deepens understanding of social and emotional skills. In this light, it is important to disrupt the bias toward extroversion that often infiltrates the performing arts and prepare everyone to equally participate in classroom role-plays. This involves waking up the kinetic modality for all learners; acknowledging and equally valuing a range of performance styles, from extremely animated to more subdued; and creating various jobs aside from acting (such as charting student ideas, calling "action," calling "freeze," and helping to set up the playing area) that students can be engaged in during role-plays.

Classrooms are not the first place we think of when we think about kinetic learning. Gymnasiums, athletic fields, and dance studios are more likely what comes to mind when we think of the kinetic learning modality. But, in classroom role-plays, everyone engages with the information on a physical level.

Neuroscience tells us that we have all sympathetic responses to the experiences of others through the work of mirror neurons. These special neurons allow us to physically feel the same things that other people do, especially if and when we observe their experiences. Recall anytime you jumped out of your seat and screamed at a horror movie at the exact same moment that the main character jumped back from the surprise onslaught of a knife-wielding evildoer. Those were your mirror neurons at work, connecting your physical experience to that of another person, in this case a fictional person whom you were observing.

With this in mind, we need to take into account the fact that all students, not just the actors, will have a kinetic learning experience during a classroom role-play. They will feel things in their bodies either because they are acting the part of a person in a conflict, or because they are observing a conflict and sympathetically relating to the experiences of the character. These bodily sensations provide contextual information for them and increase their understanding of larger themes, the characters, and the social and emotional skills being explored. So, if and when a student is asked a question like, "How was the character feeling?" they will be able to reflect upon their own sympathetic responses, as well as their observations, to inform their answer.

In order to prepare students to observe and interpret these sensations within themselves we need to wake up their kinetic learning system at the start of any classroom role-play. There are many ways to do this. After arranging your classroom in preparation for the role-play, consider using any one of these exercises to start the class. Choose a warm-up activity that seems right for the mood of your class and spend about seven minutes in physical activity.

- Allow the students to toss a soft ball around the circle, making sure that everyone receives and throws the ball at least once. Students may toss silently, or by calling one another's name. To create a challenge, see if students can remember the person they threw the ball to and who they received it from. Then have them repeat the pattern as a class. Add in another ball or two as they continue to repeat the pattern to increase the challenge.
- Present a series of prompts that will invite various students, for whom this prompt is true, to switch seats. After you have shared a few prompts to get the game going, invite students to share some prompts and invite their peers to switch seats. For instance, "Find a new seat if you are wearing stripes . . . like to cook . . . are the eldest sibling . . . are bilingual . . . play an instrument."
- Lead the students in a series of gentle stretches, or invite one or more students to lead the class in a series of stretches. Hands over head, stretching to one side, reaching over and touching the ground, balancing on one leg, and head rolls can all be effective.
- For a high-energy warm-up, consider jumping jacks or running in place or a combination of the two.
- For a more creative warm-up, invite the students to make a series of physical tableaus. A tableau is a living picture that is created by taking a physical stance that represents a feeling, activity, or idea. It can be done individually, in pairs, or in small groups. Working with tableaus engages students kinetically as well as visually. Ask students to individually create tableaus for the emotions of excitement, sadness, fear, anger, confusion, isolation, peace, happiness, and so on. Ask students to work in pairs to create tableaus for the activities of playing chess, joking around, shopping, dancing, and so on. Ask students to work in small groups to create tableaus for the ideas of cooperation, competition, resistance, justice, freedom, and so on.
- For an extra challenge, ask students to create their tableaus quickly and to change them quickly. You can cue this by calling "change" and "freeze" so that students move quickly between various tableaus.

After a kinetic warm-up for everyone in the class, we will also need to account for various performance styles in role-plays so that the widest range of students feels comfortable acting. There will always be students who want to be the "stars." It is important to resist the urge to allow any particular student to dominate. In classroom role-plays, everyone is learning more about observing behavior and practicing new skills. As such, it is important to recognize that everyone shows their emotions differently and being more dramatic does not make one student a better actor than another who may be more subdued. Remember, no one is performing in front of a traditional audience. Student actors in classroom role-plays are simply performing for each other as a form of collaborative experiential and modal learning.

So, while some students may seek the spotlight, others may shy away from it. Make a point of conveying that everyone can participate as a student actor in a classroom role-play. While more extroverted students may embody their characters with larger gestures and louder or more animated voices, more introverted students may use subtle gestures and softer voices to convey the same emotions.

The range of gestures and vocal tone that can be used to convey the same emotions are all valid, and this fact teaches us about the challenges of reading human behavior in real life. We all know people who are more naturally animated and those who are more naturally reserved. While they all experience the full range of human emotions, from joy to despair, they may look and sound quite different while they are doing it. This is the beauty of personality and of character. There is not one way to experience or express emotions that is more real or valid than another. We can learn a lot about human behavior by accepting the wide range of expression for the same emotion.

Finally, some students will never want to participate as actors, and this is fine. They can participate by:

- Helping to set up the room
- Charting student ideas for issues to explore in the role-play
- Calling "action" at the start of the role-play
- Calling "freeze" to alert the actors to pause so that the group can discuss what is happening at an interesting point in the role-play
- Calling on new actors to step into the second or third version of a role-play
- Assisting in the facilitation of peer-to-peer dialogue or group dialogue by calling on students, passing around a talking piece, or choosing equity sticks labeled with student names
- Charting student learning and reflections
- Helping to return the room to its original design

MAKING IT REAL

Classroom role-plays do not rely on prewritten scripts. The point of engaging in classroom role-plays, specifically to teach social and emotional learning, is to explore issues and conflicts in the lives of your students and allow them to practice applying social and emotional skills in the resolution of these problems. Students already have concrete experiences of difficult feelings, moments of conflict, and moments when they did not understand someone else's point of view. We can draw on these moments and use them as a rich source for concrete experiences of our content. In order to do this, we need to invite students to share various issues or conflicts they've experienced.

Opening up the classroom to discussions of a personal nature can be intimidating for everyone. Both students and teachers alike may feel scared of being vulnerable in front of others, scared of their personal issues being shared as gossip, or scared that they will be put on the spot to share more than they would like. So, it is important to have some boundaries set up around how to share issues that students have personally experienced.

First, it is important to frame the conversation around the specific social and emotional skill that will be learned and practiced in the classroom role-play. The second half of this book is dedicated to essential social and emotional learning skills and is meant to be a resource that will allow you to focus your discussion around skill building.

Before opening a discussion of student issues or problems, take time to familiarize yourself with the social and emotional learning concept that you would like to explore. Introduce the concept or skill to your students and allow them to discuss it fully. Field their questions and allow them to explore the ideas.

Then frame the invitation to discuss student experiences around the specific social and emotional skill that you have determined is the most relevant and current for your students with a question like, "Now that you have an understanding of the assertiveness skill of communicating needs, when do you think this might be useful in real life?" Help students to reflect upon their own lives and experiences with additional questions like, "Have you had an experience where this skill might have been helpful?" This will help them reflect upon their own experiences in a more focused manner and will also begin the process of scaffolding the subjective experiences of their lives onto the objective concepts of social and emotional skills.

It is also important to establish some boundaries around what can be safely shared. These boundaries will be different in different classrooms. Some classrooms encourage personal sharing and have the classroom climate, peer-to-peer relationships, and peer-to-teacher relationships to support that kind of dialogue. Others may need more boundaries. Neither is better or worse, but it is important to find the approach to personal sharing that is right for you and your class.

One protocol that can be helpful is to suggest that actual names not be used when sharing experiences about peers. So rather than saying, "Yesterday, Makeda spread gossip about me in the schoolyard and now no one will talk to me," a student might say, "Recently, another student spread gossip about me in the schoolyard and now no one will talk to me."

Another protocol that might be helpful is to suggest that students share experiences from their past rather than from their present. You also may steer students away from sharing actual stories from their lives and encourage them instead to come up with imaginative ideas for role-plays between fictionalized characters that relate to the social-emotional learning skill that you will explore as a group.

Finally, if it there is resistance to this type of personal sharing, you may present students with a variety of different scenarios that they could role-play and engage them in a dialogue about which one they prefer and why. The second half of the book provides a number of scenarios for each social and emotional skill that you and your students explore. These scenarios can be thought of as flexible role-play options; you may choose whichever seems to best match the needs and interests of your students, or you may wish to create your own scenarios and present them as options for your class.

Once you have introduced the social and emotional learning skill you will explore and set some protocols for how you would like students to engage in sharing experiences, invite a discussion, chart their answers (or have a student chart them), and look for similar themes. For example, if learning to communicate needs is the skill, a chart of students' recent experiences might include the phrases "fought with brother over remote," "fought with sister over whose turn it was to do dishes," and "felt left out at recess when I couldn't play dodgeball." Looking at a chart such as this, a teacher-facilitator might suggest that a role-play between siblings could be interesting, as more than one idea involves siblings.

CLARIFY CHARACTERS, STORY, AND SEL SKILL

While it was suggested that the SEL skill be identified first and that the brainstorm around real-life student issues would follow, it is also possible to reverse the order of these two activities. Starting with a student brainstorm about real-life issues can be an exciting way to identify a relevant SEL skill to practice in a role-play. Whichever order you choose, it is important to explicitly link the SEL skill and the student issue so that there is clarity for the actors and audience alike before the role-play begins.

Following from the example above, let's imagine that we chose to do a role-play practicing the SEL skill of stating needs as a way of addressing the issue of one sibling refusing to wash dishes. The teacher-facilitator would review the SEL skill and clarify the issue being explored. For example, "We will role-play the disagreement about two siblings fighting over whose turn it is to do the dishes. We hope to see the siblings resolve their conflict. The characters will use 'I need' statements, which begin with 'I' and state the speaker's basic needs. For instance, 'I need you to do your dishes because I have a big test tomorrow. I have to start studying.'"

It is important that you establish up front that you will do more than one version of this role-play. Presenting multiple versions allows for deeper learning of the SEL skill. It scaffolds students into higher-order thinking like comparison and analysis with the power of contrasting examples. In other words, it is easier to understand the powerful effect of applying of an SEL skill to an issue if we can observe what happens when we don't try, or when we try half-heartedly, or when one of us tries and the other resists. Seeing and understanding the gaps in communication that SEL skills can fill helps students to more deeply understand the purpose of the skills and is a powerful motivation for trying them in real life.

Multiple versions also allow the teacher-facilitator to support the deliberate practice of the SEL skill. As all limbic system learning requires practice, students must be able to practice the application of an SEL skill multiple times, receive feedback on that practice, and be motivated to improve as they are pushed out of their comfort zone by a skilled teacher-facilitator. Deliberate practice helps students gain the confidence necessary to use these skills in their own lives.

Lastly, multiple versions of a role-play invite the possibility of more students stepping into the role of actor. A different "cast" may be chosen for each version of the role-play. This avoids the trap of the class "stars" wanting to dominate the role-play format. It also provides deeper learning, as each new pairing will present a different interpretation of the characters and the issue being explored.

As you and your students become more experienced with classroom role-plays, you will come up with endless versions of a role-play that are based on different interpretations of the issue, the character's feelings, and the challenges and opportunities of using SEL skills. But, it is always good to do at least three versions of a given role-play: one version in which both characters refuse to use the SEL skill, a second version in which only one character uses the skill, and a final version in which both characters apply the use of the SEL skill to the issue being explored.

EVERYONE HAS A JOB

Assign the actors character names and make sure they understand their roles. Even if students are role-playing a situation that's based on real life, it's important that the real names of the participants not be used. This will help everyone focus on the problem being explored, not the people involved. Separating the person from the problem is a key component of conflict resolution, and we want to reinforce this by making sure to use character names.

Make sure that the audience knows that they have a job as well. The job of the audience is to observe the role-play and think about the SEL learning targets, to engage in discussion about what they observed and how things could have gone differently, to make suggestions about how the characters could act differently in a subsequent version, and perhaps to volunteer to step in as an actor.

You may also assign additional jobs to various students. This can help with engagement, especially for students who may be hesitant about participating in group discussions or acting. Valid ways of contributing include charting student ideas for issues to explore in the role-play; calling "action" at the start of the role-play; calling "freeze" to alert the actors to pause so that the group can discuss what is happening at an interesting point in the role-play; calling on new actors to step into the second or third version of a role-play; assisting in the facilitation of peer-to-peer dialogue or group dialogue by calling on students, passing around a talking piece, or choosing equity sticks labeled with student names; and charting student learning and reflections.

ACTOR PREPARATION: NOTE ON IMPROVISATION

Students will not be working from a prewritten script. They will be improvising the scene based on their understanding of the issues, the characters, and the SEL skill that they are practicing. This can be intimidating at first, as our associations with performance are linked to the idea of the perfect performance of a prewritten script. This brings up feelings about saying the wrong line and looking foolish or needing to memorize lines before you can act a character. Alternatively, it can be intimidating to think about coming up with your character lines on the spot. So, the more we can move away from the idea of performance and move toward the idea of creative collaboration the better our classroom role-plays will go.

Improvisation can be introduced as a conversation between fictional characters. We all have conversations every day of our lives. Most of us have some basic conversational skills under our belts already. With improvisation, we simply translate these skills to a fictionalized situation between fictionalized characters. Once we get past the fear of not knowing what we should say ahead of time, improvisation is actually less difficult than memorizing a script because there literally is no wrong line. Once students understand that they have the freedom to create their own lines and their own characters through improvisation, a large number of them will gravitate to this exciting activity.

To prepare them, model an improvised conversation with one of your more loquacious students or with a co-teacher. Introduce the idea that improvising is just engaging in a conversation as two fictional people in a fictional situation. When we improvise we imagine what our character would be feeling in the situation, and we use the conversation skills we already have to speak as we believe they would. Choose a simple situation and characters. For example, two people stand in line at the grocery store and get their items confused on the counter. Allow a student to call "action," and begin your improvised conversation.

Students can then work on these same skills in pairs. Present them with a similarly simple situation, such as two students who are standing on the lunch line and one of them cuts in front of the other. Call "action" and allow all student pairs to improvise a conversation. The room will be loud and a bit chaotic, but everyone should come away with an idea of how easy improvisation can be.

You can repeat this exercise, with various situations, as a kind of verbal and auditory warm-up akin to the kinetic warm-up suggested earlier. You might follow a kinetic warm-up with this activity to allow everyone to warm up their verbal and auditory skills and to give all your students equal practice time in developing comfort with improvisation. We all have the ability to improvise in classroom role-plays; it is just a matter of recognizing the conversation skills we already have and applying them to fictional situations.

ACTOR PREPARATION: STEPPING INTO THE SCENE

Once actors have been chosen for the role-plays, make sure they are prepared. They should understand the issue, the SEL skill, the version of the role-play they will enact and their part in it, the feelings their character may be experiencing, and a starting line for their character. While this may sound like a lot, we can support student actors in this preparation fairly easily with a few simple questions. These preparation questions may be asked by the teacher-facilitator or students in the class.

As a classroom role-play is not a performance or a show, but a creative collaboration in experiential and modal learning, helping to prepare the actors is part of the learning experience for everyone involved. The preparation questions will help everyone to understand the issues and SEL skills more deeply, allow students to contribute directly to one another's learning, and create an atmosphere of support rather than the atmosphere of competition that often surrounds performance. Use these simple questions to prepare your student actors to role-play:

- How would you paraphrase the issue we will explore?
- How do you think your character is feeling?
- How will the SEL skill we practice help resolve the issue?
- In this version, will your character use this skill?
- What will your first line be?

Though it is not necessary to have an acting background to engage in improvisational role-plays, some students may come to class with a bit of acting experience or a deeper interest in performing. These students may want to do a little more preparation before engaging in the role-play. Alternatively, you might feel a little extra preparation would be helpful as a general practice.

In this case, student actors could be given a few minutes to prepare on their own. This might be done outside the circle or horseshoe or in the hallway. While the actors are engaged in this more in-depth preparation, the group can discuss the themes of the role-play in greater detail in preparation for their job of watching and listening closely, and coming up with alternative approaches to solving the problem. The actors might:

- Decide on the first four to six lines of the improvisation, rather than just the first two lines.
- Think about the quality of their character's voice. Do they speak quickly or slowly? Do they speak loudly or softly? What emotion is conveyed in the tone of their character's voice?
- Think about the use of their bodies in the improvisation. Will their character sit or stand? Will they move quickly or slowly? Will they keep their distance from their scene partner or will the audience see them interact more physically? Which of these choices best conveys the character?

Finally, a classroom role-play is a creative collaboration that is meant to stimulate discussion about the use of social and emotional skills. Of course, we can assume that there will be discussion at the conclusion of a role-play. But, it can be very effective to have discussion during the course of a role-play, as well.

One way to do this is to call "freeze" at moments of heightened vocal and physical expression. After the teacher-facilitator or a student helper calls "freeze," the actors will hold their facial expressions and bodies in stillness and will stop speaking. Their stillness will create a visual tableau of the issue or conflict, much like the exercise that the students may have practiced in their kinetic warm-up. As a teacher-facilitator, you can use this tableau as a visual learning aid for asking higher-order thinking questions.

This is a somewhat advanced role-play skill and may be something that you would want to try after students are comfortable with role-plays. Before they enter the playing area, make sure to let your actors know whether you will be using this technique to further discussion or will want them to complete the scene before discussion begins.

PREPPING THE AUDIENCE

Your audience will be looking for clues to the feeling and motivations of the characters in the role-play, evidence that helps them interpret the themes and conflicts, and ideas for alternative ways to solve the problem between the characters. So, it can be helpful to alert them to things to watch and listen for. You may want to pose a series of open-ended questions while the actors are preparing, during a "freeze," or at the end of the role-play to explore the communicative power of role-play performances and how they influence our interpretation of the themes and story. For instance:

- If a character repeats the same line more than once, what might they be feeling/thinking?
- If a character avoids a question, what might they be feeling/thinking?
- If a character uses accusations, what might they be feeling/thinking?
- If a character is bargaining or presenting various options, what might they be feeling/thinking?
- If a character raises their voice, speaks softly, speaks quickly, or hesitates to speak, what might they be feeling/thinking?
- If a character leans in closer, what might they be feeling/thinking?
- If a character's posture deflates, what might they be feeling/thinking?
- If a character walks away, what might they be feeling/thinking?
- If a character moves quickly or slowly, what might they be feeling/thinking?

RUNNING A ROLE-PLAY

After you have fully prepared your actors, ask them to enter the playing area, be it the center of a circle, the open end of a horseshoe, or another space that you have created. They should position themselves, both the shape of their body and its placement in the space, in a way that captures the feelings that their character has at the start of the scene. They should stand fairly still and wait for the audience to silence themselves and ready themselves to watch and listen. When both the actors and audience are ready to begin, have a student call "action" to start the role-play.

As you watch the role-play, keep the problem and the SEL learning targets in mind. Watch the actors' bodies closely. Listen carefully to the words they choose. If you are letting the role-play run to completion, you may want to make mental notes, or actual written notes, of moments of heightened conflict, moments when the SEL skill was used, and moments when there was a shift in dynamic between the characters. You may also want to jot down questions that you feel will promote discussion.

If you would like the students to engage in discussion during the course of the role-play, watch the actors' bodies and listen to their words carefully. At a moment of heightened physical and vocal expression, call "freeze" (or signal for a student helper to do so). The actors will hold their faces and bodies in stillness, creating a tableau. As they maintain this hold, you can ask higher-order thinking questions to promote student engagement and understanding.

For example, as the student actors role-play the scenario exploring whose turn it is to do the dishes, one actor might raise her voice and point at the other, saying, "You always leave it to me!" At this precise moment, the teacher-facilitator or student helper could call "freeze." The student actors would remain frozen during this short discussion, as their bodies are now providing a visual learning aid to which other students may refer during the discussion. The teacher-facilitator, or a student facilitator, could then ask the audience members to describe:

- the body language of the characters they observed and what it conveyed
- the vocal tone they heard and what it conveyed
- what each character was feeling/thinking and why
- what each character wants and why
- what each character needs and why
- what these characters could do or say differently that might lead to a more positive outcome and better fulfill their own and each other's needs
- what SEL skills these characters could employ to improve their communication and resolve their problem
- a number of different approaches that could work and which ones the actors should role-play

After engaging in a back-and-forth dialogue about audience observations, predictions, and analysis, ask a student to call "action" and allow the actors to finish the scene. When the scene is finished, reflect together on the choices the characters made, how things might have gone differently, and what version the class would like to role-play next.

Whether you break the scene for discussion with a "freeze" or allow it to play to its natural conclusion, it is important to discuss the interaction between the characters and the feelings expressed, the effectiveness of the SEL skill, and alternate versions of the role-play to explore other facets of this same issue.

REFINE, REVISE, REDO

At the conclusion of a performance or a show, the audience claps in appreciation and goes home, hopefully feeling like they "got their money's worth" because they were adequately entertained. The conclusion of a classroom role-play is when the real learning begins. It is when discussion develops, collaboration expands, and practice deepens.

As practice is a key component of limbic system learning and as deliberate practice, where students are pushed out of their comfort zone, is the most effective type of practice, it is essential that we refine, revise, and redo each classroom role-play more than once. This allows more students to step into the role of actor, and allows everyone to push their thinking to imagine the many different ways an SEL skill can be applied to a given problem.

As mentioned previously, a simple way to generate various versions of a role-play is to have the first version of the role-play be one where none of the characters uses the SEL skill being explored, the second version of the role-play be one where one character uses the skill, and the third version be one where both (or all, should there be more than two) characters use the skill. Once you and the students get the hang of role-plays, there are many ways to generate alternate versions and push student thinking with more higher-order thinking questions that invite students to analyze and synthesize the information.

The questions that you might ask to push student thinking about alternate versions of the role-play will depend on the issues being explored and the SEL skill you are practicing. For example, in exploring the use of "I need" statements to help two siblings in a disagreement over who should do the dishes, here are some questions that, if explored fully, might lead to alternate versions of that role-play.

- How did this approach work for character 1? Did they get what they wanted?
- Shall we try an alternate version where character 2 gives character 1 what he/she wants?
- How did this approach work for character 2? Did they get what they wanted?
- Shall we try an alternate version where character 1 makes an effort to change their behavior toward character 2?
- What could they have done differently to produce a more positive outcome?
- How might this go if the characters used self-talk to cool down before delivering their "I need" statements?
- Shall we try an alternate version where both characters practice self-talk before delivering their "I need" statements?
- How might this go if the characters used a softer tone of voice?
- Shall we try an alternate version where both characters use a different tone of voice?

After you and the class have chosen an alternate version that you would like to explore, choose different actors, a different student helper to call "action," and a different student helper to call "freeze" should you decide to stop midway for a discussion. This will distribute the active engagement across as many members of the class as possible and will also reinforce the idea that there is always more than one way to look at an issue, conflict, or problem.

EVERYBODY PRACTICES

After various versions of the role-play have been enacted and the class has fully discussed their learning, we need to make sure that all students get a chance to practice the SEL skill being explored. Referring back to our introduction to improvisation, one of the easiest and most effective ways to practice an SEL skill is in the context of an improvised conversation.

Have students work in pairs or small groups at their seats. Allow them to choose any of the versions of the role-play that they have just watched and discussed, or to create a new version with their partner. Alternately, after watching multiple versions of a role-play using a specific skill applied to specific issue, it can also be exciting to ask student pairs to come up with an altogether different situation in which the same SEL skill could be applied.

For instance, rather than using an "I need" statement to address the issue of whose turn it is to do dishes, students might decide to engage in an improvised conversation that incorporates "I need" statements between two friends who want to do different things over the weekend. When all partners are clear about which version they will explore, call "action" and let the students improvise a conversation that involves the use of the SEL skill.

This is essentially a role-play that is done from their seats, rather than in the playing area. Alternatively, if you have space you could invite the pairs or small groups to spread out across the available space and find their own personal playing area. Make sure that each pair has enough room to interact without interfering with the work of their peers. Then invite all pairs to enact the role-play in a more full-bodied manner. Whether seated or standing and fully engaged physically, peer-to-peer improvised conversations allow everyone to practice the SEL skill and to translate what they saw and heard during the role-play into their own bodies, minds, and voices.

While the classroom will be noisy and may seem chaotic, this practice is essential. All students need a chance to try out the SEL skill in the context of a conversation in order to build the confidence needed to use it in their lives. Only by trying it out with their own voices and bodies can this confidence begin to develop.

As we learned earlier, feedback on our practice is essential in order to learn and grow. Providing feedback during pair or small group practice can be challenging. A teacher-facilitator can walk around the room and provide feedback to pairs or small groups, though it will be hard to do this equally for everyone.

One solution is to have students provide feedback to one another. For instance, pairs could do two versions of a role-play, where characters alternate in their use of the SEL skill being practiced. At the conclusion of each version, the student whose character did not use the SEL skill can give their partner feedback on their use of the SEL skill in the role-play.

Students may need some guidance around how to give one another useful feedback on their SEL skill practice. First, make sure that the SEL skill being practiced is clear to everyone. Returning to our working example, we might remind students that "I need" statements begin with "I" and state the speaker's basic needs. For instance, "I need you to do your dishes because I have to study for a big test tomorrow."

Then provide students with simple guidelines for supporting each other in practicing that skill. A simple set of observations and questions that students could use to support one another can be helpful. For example:

- I'm not sure I understood your "I need" statement. Let me try to paraphrase what I heard and maybe we can understand it better together.
- I understood your "I need" statement and it helped me understand how your character was feeling and what my character should do to make things better.
- Why did you choose this "I need" statement for your character?
- Is there another "I need" statement that your character might have delivered?

After all pairs have had a chance to practice and receive feedback on their practice, either from you or their practice partner, invite the students to share their level of confidence in using this SEL skill in their real lives. Ask if they have a situation in their real lives where they might want to use the SEL skill. Ask if they feel confident doing that now or if they will need more practice. Ask how they plan to practice. Will they work with a friend? Will they work alone? Would they like support in their practice from you directly?

WRAPPING IT UP

Because the learning that is done during a classroom role-play is so different than the learning that is done in most academic subjects, it is important to "close" the session. A closing helps students to transition from the experiential and modal learning of the classroom role-play to the method of teaching and learning that will be required of them during the other parts of their day. A closing can be a simple acknowledgment of work well done, a sharing of high points in the lesson, a quick charting of ideas for the next session, or a moment of silence. Choose a closing that you feel will help your students transition out of this work and into their next learning environment. You may want to pose some final evaluative questions, such as:

- Of all the approaches we role-played, which one worked best and why?
- What can we all learn from these role-plays about how to handle similar situations in our own lives?
- Can you think of a situation in your own life where the skills we learned today would be helpful?

CONCLUSION

A classroom role-play is a form of collaborative experiential and modal learning. The audience and actors engage in Kolb's four stages of experiential learning by sharing personal experiences to explore in a role-play, observing and reflecting upon what happens in the role-play, conceptualizing alternative outcomes for the characters, and experimenting with the application of various social and emotional learning skills to the issue being explored. Students are supported in their learning by the additional information that they receive through the auditory, kinetic, and visual modalities encompassed in role-plays and by the guidance of a teacher-facilitator who pushes them out of their comfort zone as they practice these skills.

As social and emotional learning itself takes place in the limbic system, and limbic system learning requires practice, one-on-one feedback, and positive motivation, students will repeatedly practice the skills they learn. As we know that deliberate practice, where students are pushed beyond their comfort zone, creates the deepest learning, we will deliberately build practice and feedback into our classroom role-plays by doing multiple version of the same role-play, allowing for group practice of SEL skills, and supporting teacher-to-student and peer-to-peer feedback.

We are now familiar with the basic steps for creating an effective classroom role-play—from setting the playing area to waking up kinetic and auditory awareness, from pairing real-life issues with SEL skills to prep actors, from improvising to group practice. Whatever the content of the role-play itself or the SEL skill being practiced, this basic form can be followed.

In addition, as we become more comfortable in the role of teacher-facilitator of classroom role-plays, we can make adjustments to this form to suit our own teaching style and the needs and interests of our students. It is also worth mentioning that while this book is dedicated to using classroom role-plays to teach social and emotional learning, classroom role-plays may be used to enhance learning in a wide range of subject areas, from social studies to history, to civics, to literature, and even to science. Once the basic form and structure of a classroom role-play are mastered, they can be used to explore everything from the imagined lives of escaped slaves on the Underground Railroad, to alternative endings for students' favorite books, to the failed early experiments of well-known scientists.

There are many different aspects of the basic role-play format. It can take a while to feel comfortable facilitating all of them, and the role of the teacher-facilitator in classroom role-plays is quite different than that of a teacher in a traditional subject area classroom. In addition, each aspect of the role-play format is enhanced by a different type of facilitation. So, it is important to have a wealth of facilitation skills to draw from in order to best facilitate this kind of learning. Let's take a deeper look at the art of facilitation, in order to help us move through the elements of classroom role-play with greater ease and clarity.

THREE

Facilitating Collaborative, Creative, and Experiential Learning

Pre-K classrooms look quite different than most of their elementary and secondary counterparts. Oftentimes they are full of guided play, which is absent in most elementary or secondary schools, unless they are dedicated to experiential or project-based learning.

Teachers in pre-K classrooms typically spend a short amount of time in traditional teacher presentation mode, and much more time encouraging students to work in centers, which are dedicated to collaborative, creative, and experiential learning. Students often choose which center they would like to visit and there is always a center dedicated to imaginative play, a close counterpart to role-plays.

Teachers travel around the room in the role of a teacher-facilitator supporting student-driven learning with questions and dialogue prompts. These questions and prompts help to focus the guided play and ensure that students progress toward a learning goal while they are working, in large part, joyfully and independently. As a result, pre-K classrooms have retained a joy in learning that elementary and secondary classrooms often lose in the high-stakes testing culture that has infiltrated our schools.

But, let's be honest, it is easier to give pre-K students collaborative, creative, and experiential learning opportunities than it is to do so for older students. First of all, pre-K students are smaller, and creating experiential learning centers is much easier when working with little bodies. Developmentally, pre-K students are drawn to imaginative play as well as seeking adult approval. And, since their vocabulary is limited, the time it takes to engage them in collaborative and creative discussion is reduced in comparison to the time investment required to engage older students in the same kinds of discussions.

35

As students age they have larger vocabularies, more independent ideas, and less interest in adult approval. And, of course, creating something akin to pre-K experiential learning centers for elementary and secondary students is a challenge due to space constraints. All of the developmental changes as students grow older create challenges for teachers who may want to facilitate collaborative, creative, and experiential learning activities for their students. In addition, as academic pressures increase, teachers and students all feel the time constraints of preparing for testing, and collaborative, creative, and experiential learning opportunities for older students often fall by the wayside.

But the benefits of these kind of learning experiences, of which social and emotional learning role-plays are one, are great. So, it is worth taking time to look more closely at some of the challenges and pitfalls of organizing and facilitating creative, collaborative, and experiential learning activities for older students and to think about ways that we can "up" our facilitation game.

COMPLEX AND CREATIVE FACILITATION

In the simplest sense, facilitation can be described as any set of techniques that are used to enhance group engagement, effectiveness, and learning. Unlike traditional teaching or lecturing, teacher-facilitators are equal participants in a group process for which they are advocates. As process advocates, teacher-facilitators may use a number of different techniques to create buy-in and agreement, encourage group experimentation, and spread leadership and engagement across all group members.

Most teachers already use some facilitation techniques in their classrooms. Depending on the subject matter and the lesson, we might use fairly simple facilitation tools, such as asking contingent follow-up questions after a read-aloud passage. We may draw from the Socratic method when facilitating group discussions by presenting a topic; encouraging direct peer-to-peer discussion among students; and clarifying, synthesizing, and restating earlier opinions to help keep the focus on the discussion as it develops. Or, we might use more multistep and complex facilitation tools, as when we are facilitating a complicated group project in a short period of time. While we can certainly bring to bear all of our facilitation techniques in social and emotional learning role-plays, creative and collaborative experiential learning can present some extra challenges.

If we want to use role-plays to teach social and emotional learning skills, we need to take a closer look at the complex facilitation techniques that will allow us to support collaboration, creation, and a depth of experiential learning in the classroom. To start imagining the possibilities of complex and creative facilitation, it might be helpful to look at an example from the real world.

Lawrence "Butch" Morris was an American composer and conductor who created a complex form of facilitated improvisation called Conduction. Morris worked with small orchestras composed of musicians playing classical orchestral instruments, like violin and cello, as well as rock and jazz instruments, such as electric guitar and drums.

Rather than give musicians a written score to "read down" while he conducted their interpretation of that score, as a traditional conductor would, Morris invited musicians to improvise the musical content itself. Imagine five to twenty-five musicians deciding to play whatever they wanted, whenever they wanted. Does this conjure an image of the creative cacophony that can sometimes occur in our classrooms?

What Morris and his musicians were able to do with that cacophony, how he was able to shape the individual offerings of a wide array of creative people, is a fascinating example of complex and creative facilitation. By devising a system of hand gestures, he and his musicians were able to make orchestral music out of the creative impulses of the players. One gesture communicated that Morris liked and wanted to save an improvised phrase, another communicated that players could repeat and memorize that phrase, another invited players to embellish that phrase, and a host of other gestures allowed Morris to suggest entrances, exits, repeats, and volume changes. The resulting music was both inclusive of the individual voices in the group and larger than them. It was also beautiful.

The ability to relinquish control, listen deeply, and follow the lead of the participants are facilitation skills that both pre-K teachers and Butch Morris embody in unique and powerful ways. Though we may not have the flexibility to set up independent experiential learning centers in our classrooms the way pre-K teachers do or the need to develop a complex set of hand gestures to shape a creative dialogue with our students, like Mr. Morris did with his musicians, a closer look at the need to relinquish control, listen deeply, and follow student leads could help us fine-tune the facilitation skills we already have. In order to support collaborative, creative, and experiential learning during social and emotional learning role-plays, we need to take an adventurous dive into the possibilities of complex facilitation.

RELINQUISH CONTROL

In chapter 1, we talked about the ancient quote that forms the basis for experiential learning: "For the things we have to learn before we can do them, we learn by doing them." Social and emotional learning role-plays are a form of experiential learning where students learn about social and emotional skills through the experience of role-plays and the deliberate practice of the skills explored in the role-plays.

With any and all experiential learning—be it the guided play of pre-K classrooms, the musical explorations of Butch Morris and his musicians, the project-based learning examples shared in chapter 1, or athletics—the participants and the teacher-facilitators understand that learning simply cannot happen without doing. The deeper the experience of doing, especially if it includes repeated and deliberate practice, the deeper the learning. Yet, the way we are often trained as teachers makes it difficult for us to comfortably allow students to learn by doing.

This is not our fault. Hundreds of years of habitual approaches to pedagogy center the teacher's voice and presentation style. In general, Western education promotes the value of teacher controls and passive learning. Students are often graded on how well they submit to this pedagogical style, rather than being graded on qualities that actually influence their learning such as persistence, curiosity, passion, imagination, productivity, or talent. It is easy to see that our history and cultural biases make it hard to relinquish control and allow students to learn by doing.

Of course, in certain situations, such as test preparation, introductions to new information, or rote learning tasks, there is great value to a more traditional approach to teaching. But top-down, traditional, and teacher-centered approaches will simply not serve us or our students when we are engaging in collaborative, creative, experiential learning activities such as social and emotional learning role-plays. In situations where the best way to learn is by doing, we need to relinquish some control and turn our focus to facilitating collaboration, creation, and experience. We need to relinquish control to make space for the unique and individual experiences and points of view of our students. We need to learn the art of facilitating without dominating.

The Dominant Teacher

Teachers are often talkers. If we are not naturally so, we may be encouraged to find the part of ourselves that can be pushed to the extrovert side of the introvert-extrovert continuum as part of our teacher training. Teachers are judged on everything—from their classroom climate skills, presentation skills, and knowledge and delivery of content to their behavior management skills—based on the actual words that they say, or fail to say, in a given classroom period. In traditional instruction, the teacher's voice is the main medium for communicating. Therefore, their voice, as opposed to the individual and collective voices of their students, is dominant.

As a result of years of traditional pedagogy that emphasizes the dominant voice of teachers, and praises that dominance as good teaching, many teachers often present themselves, consciously or unconsciously, as the keepers of knowledge. We transmit this knowledge, often through passive instruction. We expect students to receive it and regurgitate it in some form, whether through answering a question, writing a paper that demonstrates their knowledge, or submitting to some kind of assessment that tests the retention of that knowledge. In these traditional approaches to teaching, the teacher is in control, the students are expected to follow their lead, and learning is, in large part, a passive process.

In traditional instruction, there is an implied, albeit highly controlled, one-on-one relationship between the instructor and each student in the class. Because students are expected to speak only if they are spoken to and only in response to what is asked of them by the instructor, the tone of each one-on-one exchange is determined by the question the instructor asks and the student's ability to answer that question.

The relationship between the instructor and each student often hinges upon a student's ability to answer the instructor's question not only accurately, but in a tone that mirrors that of the instructor. In this very prescribed manner, traditional instruction is often a series of orchestrated, one-on-one exchanges, at the center of which you will find the teacher.

In fact, in traditional, top-down instruction, the teacher is the most engaged person in the classroom, as no one else can actively engage in the lesson unless they engage directly with the teacher. While these individual relationships between teacher and student are highlighted and controlled rigidly by the teacher, the group is expected to be silent. The group, and all of the relationships it contains, is an unacknowledged and passive presence.

We all remember being asked to raise our hands, after a lecture of some sort, in order to answer a teacher's question. If we called out without raising our hands, there may have been consequences. If we failed to raise our hands often enough, there may have been consequences. If we raised our hands when we were supposed to and did it often enough, but failed to provide an answer that pleased our teacher, there may have been consequences. Many of us decided to stop raising our hands because there were more chances that we would be dismissed as a result of doing so than there were chances that we would be acknowledged.

Because there was often only one way to engage, by raising our hands, we might have experienced an atmosphere where competition festered between the students who were always first to raise their hand and those who refrained from doing so for reasons ranging from boredom, to shyness, to having learning styles that respond better to other types of instruction. We may have wanted to engage but couldn't compete with the students who always were first to raise their hands, or the students who always seemed to have the "right" answer. With no other avenue for engagement, we may have become disengaged, especially if we did not fall into the "always first" or "always right" category of students.

We were all, at one time, students. We all know where we fit on the continuum of hand-raisers to back-of-the-class note-passers, and we probably know exactly why we landed where we did on that continuum of engagement. While certain age groups are more receptive to a traditional instruction style than others, and certain subject areas lend themselves to a traditional instruction style more easily than others, we all know from the experience of being students ourselves that traditional instruction—silent room, passive instruction, and raised hands—is no guarantee of engagement or learning.

While the most extreme version of this style is falling out of fashion, it still exists in many of our classrooms. And, a less extreme version of this, where a teacher may give students a chance to turn and talk or to work occasionally in groups, may still use this traditional approach to pedagogy as a base. This is true even in classrooms and schools that consider themselves to be progressive.

Whether we want to acknowledge it or not, much of a teacher's time and energy in traditional instruction, or less rigid but traditionally influenced instruction, is spent controlling student behavior so that it fits into a very narrow and prescribed range. It is assumed that this narrow range will best promote learning and that teachers who are able to achieve the look and sound of this prescribed range of behavior in their students are also doing the best teaching. And, it is assumed that students must be doing their best learning. But, as we all know from being students ourselves, this is not necessarily the case.

In essence, there is very little room for learning by doing in a classroom where the teacher voice is dominant and the controls of student voice are rigid. For a subject such as social and emotional learning, and for a creative learning modality such as role-plays, a silent room, passive instruction, and rigid controls around when students can and cannot speak will not serve us or our students well.

Making Room for Student Voices

How can we learn to relinquish control both by diminishing the dominance of our own voices and by becoming less rigid about controlling the individual and collective voices of our students? In a general sense, how is the work of a teacher-facilitator of collaborative, creative, and experiential learning different than that of a more traditional instructor? A teacher-facilitator of collaborative, creative, and experiential learning:

- Is both a participating member and an observer of the group itself
- Does not rigidly control when students can speak
- Remains neutral and does not dominate discussion with their own opinions

- Listens to and observes all group members and creates avenues for their interactions with one another
- Is not the focal point of all interactions but rather the connective tissue that supports a multitude of peer-to-peer interactions within the group
- Refrains from demonstrating, except when absolutely necessary, and encourages students to take risks in their own practice
- Refrains from providing answers or explanations, except when absolutely necessary, and encourages students to talk among themselves to solve problems and answer questions
- Provides feedback on student practice that is neutral and observational rather than critical and global

  - Neutral and observational: "I noticed that in this role-play you chose to use the skill of self-talk right at the moment your character was triggered. Can you tell us why?"
  - Critical and global: "That's not what I asked you to do. The point of role-plays is for you to practice what I asked you to."

In contrast to traditional instruction, a teacher-facilitator of collaborative and creative experiential learning actively supports and helps to shape the ideas that emerge from within a group of which they are also a part. By putting their attention on the group and the interactions within it, the teacher-facilitator supports the group rather than controlling it. In this role, the teacher-facilitator supports students as they take risks, engage in deep inquiry, develop creative ideas collaboratively, offer one another feedback, take charge of facilitating their own dialogue, and contribute to decisions that shape the content of the class. In doing so, a teacher-facilitator supports group members as they take charge of their own learning.

Here are some simple tips for relinquishing control of the dialogue in the classroom and making space for students to learn by doing during social and emotional learning role-plays.

Advocate for the Group Process

- Join your students in a circle or half-moon classroom design. Do not choose a seat that is central or more important, and sit at their level.
- Aim to have your talking time take up 10 to 20 percent of the overall class talking time and the individual and collective student voice take up 80 to 90 percent of the overall class talking time.
- Monitor verbal and nonverbal behavior and look for signs of confusion, boredom, anger, etc. Neutrally re-engage these students with eye contact or by asking questions about their thinking.

- Monitor the tone of the dialogue and provide gentle reminders that students should respect the differences of opinion, points of view, and identities that exist within any group.
- Remind students that not everyone agrees and that this is fine. We can disagree and still be contributing members of the same group.
- Encourage students to speak directly to and with one another and do not interrupt the progressive, contingent, back-and-forth exchange of student ideas.
- Encourage back-and-forth exchanges between two or more students and do not intervene. Allow the dialogue to build and allow other students to enter it as they see fit.
- Sensitively time reflection, clarification, and synthesis statements so that they capture the cumulative ideas of the group, rather than interrupt the flow and progression of those ideas. For instance, if students are sharing various points of view on police brutality, do not interrupt their discussion or take sides. Wait until all interested students have had a chance to share and neutrally summarize by saying, "This is a difficult topic, and we have heard contrasting points of view . . ."
- Read the energy of the group and follow their wisdom. They will reveal their interests as you listen with an open mind.

Provide Scaffolding for the Group Process

- Teach students about higher-order thinking questions and encourage them to ask such questions to each other during their discussion. For instance, explicitly teach students the difference between comparison questions, prediction questions, hypothesis questions, synthesis questions, and analysis questions. Create a chart that defines each type of question so that students can refer to it when they ask one another questions.
- Give students control of the flow of dialogue by allowing them to use equity sticks, a talking piece, a soft ball that is tossed from student to student, or simply their own eye contact as a way to distribute dialogue among themselves.
- Let students refocus the group discussion on the question at hand by having them restate the question and paraphrase the answers that have been shared or make reflection, clarification, and synthesis statements that capture the flow and progression of student ideas.
- Allow students to incorporate peer-to-peer dialogue and small-group dialogue and to create their own pairs or teams.
- Allow students to choose the roles they wish to play in a role-play situation.

- Create neutral systems for making group decisions, such as an anonymous vote or a show of hands. Allow students to control these systems and to make their own decisions as a group.

Practice Neutrality and Self-Management

- Remain neutral and put your attention on advocating for the group process rather than judging student answers.
- Become more curious about student thinking and ideas, even those ideas with which you do not agree.
- Rather than correcting student ideas with which you do not agree, ask yourself if your own biases are clouding your understanding of their ideas. Seek to understand their ideas rather than judge them.
- If students are behaving in a way that disrupts the group, resist the urge to scold them harshly. Suggest that their peers ask them open-ended questions about how they are feeling and that their peers invite them to participate in a way that moves the dialogue forward.
- If a student persists in disrupting the group, after the positive intervention of their peers, suggest that the student remove themselves for three to five minutes to practice some self-management techniques such as deep breathing, stretching, meditating, or writing down their feelings in a journal. Allow them to privately manage their own behavior for three to five minutes and return to the group when they are ready.
- If a student persists in disrupting the group, even after practicing personal and private self-management, allow the group to continue their work while you speak to the student one-on-one about what they need to do in order to participate as a productive member of the group.

Trusting Students

This process of relinquishing control can be scary for everyone. Both teachers and students may feel awkward, and there may be many pregnant pauses in your discussion. These moments may be triggering. You may want to take the reins and get things moving. You may want to forgo the discomfort for familiar control. But, if we can support ourselves and our students through this discomfort, we will all develop the skills necessary to have more equitable classroom discussions and role-plays where student voices are truly centered and honored.

We must trust the ability of our students to manage their own behavior as individuals and as a group. We can build this trust by practicing new forms of dialogue that give students greater agency and supporting their ability to speak respectfully to one another. We can also teach some simple self-management techniques—such as meditating, deep breathing, and stretching—and allow them to use these techniques to manage their feelings whenever the need arises.

We need to be confident in our students' ability to control the flow and progression of dialogue with minimal intervention. We can build this confidence in ourselves and in our students by teaching them techniques for distributing dialogue, such as using equity sticks, using a talking piece, using eye contact, working in pairs or groups, or simply allowing them to call on one another. Once students understand how to facilitate the use of these techniques on their own, we can step back and allow them to take charge of using these techniques in the classroom.

We need to be confident in our students' ability to question one another and push one another's thinking. We can build this confidence by teaching them what open-ended and higher-order thinking questions are. We can allow them to practice these types of questions in low-stakes dialogue before asking them to use them in a large-group discussion.

As we are scaffolding these skills in a way that meets the needs of our students and practicing the handoff of control from ourselves to our students, we may still experience bumps in the road. The habits of traditional, top-down instruction are deeply ingrained in us all. One way to move through the discomfort is to simply acknowledge it and become comfortable with it. Consider saying something like, "It can be uncomfortable when there is silence in a group, and it is okay to feel uncomfortable. Let's all take a deep breath and see if anything shifts for us." This could be just the trick to get the conversation rolling again. If acknowledging the silence does not shift the group engagement, you may want to suggest that someone paraphrase the conversation up to this point. Then you, or a student, could pose an open-ended question to help the group re-enter the conversation.

Once our students are prepared to exercise greater agency over the flow of their own dialogue and role-plays, we can comfortably relinquish some of the controls of a traditional classroom that emphasize our voice as teachers, place us at the center of a multitude of one-on-one interactions, and silence the voice of the group. When this handoff of power takes root in our classroom, we may experience a shift in our own habits of mind as we discover how much time and space we now have to engage in the process of deep listening.

LISTEN DEEPLY

The way pre-K teachers listen to their students as they are in the midst of play-based experiential learning and the way Butch Morris listened to his musicians as they improvised have something in common. Pre-K teachers are experts at asking questions in a nondisruptive way that supports the continuation of guided play, rather than stopping it, critiquing it, or controlling it. Mr. Morris centered the voices of his musicians in much the same way as he listened intently and offered creative suggestions that did not disrupt their improvisation but rather helped them to shape it collaboratively.

Both the pre-K teachers and Butch Morris trusted the inherent autonomy and creativity of their group and the individuals comprising it. Because they trusted that their group could collaborate and generate their own creative content, they were free to listen with deep curiosity and to appreciate the stories, ideas, and music being created. In essence, because their groups were taking creative risks in their own collaboration, the teachers and Mr. Morris were able to take their own risks by listening deeply with noncritical ears and allowing themselves to be influenced and inspired by the ideas of the group.

Teachers already have many pedagogical tools to increase student dialogue and engagement. We've mentioned many of them, such as:

- Turning and talking in partnerships
- Using equity sticks to call students by name
- Using a talking piece to distribute dialogue
- Engaging in feedback loops and back-and-forth exchanges to explore student thinking
- Asking students to explain their thinking and engage in metacognition
- Having students ask one another follow-up questions
- Engaging students in group conversations
- Asking students to paraphrase the content of their group dialogue

These are all powerful techniques for increasing student dialogue. They also can be used to increase student autonomy by allowing the students themselves to facilitate these pedagogical forms, as is suggested in the section on relinquishing control. If students themselves facilitate these structures, this will allow teachers a chance to do just the kind of deep, nondisruptive, and creative listening demonstrated by our pre-K teachers and Mr. Morris. But, this doesn't always happen.

Sometimes a teacher catches up on their lesson planning while students turn and talk. Sometimes a teacher listens to a student explain their thinking, disagrees with what a student shares, and decides to abruptly move on. Sometimes a teacher who uses equity sticks to call on students by name chooses a student who triggers them, and decides to put the stick back and call on another student. Sometimes a teacher listens to a student paraphrase their peer's thinking and criticizes the student for their lack of understanding. Sometimes a teacher interrupts the flow of peer-to-peer dialogue to insert their own ideas.

In essence, sometimes teachers decide to use techniques that center student voice, but fail to become interested in listening to the content of student voices. They may be using techniques to increase student voice and autonomy, but facilitating these techniques with a top-down, traditional, and teacher-centered pedagogical style.

Even teachers who are very skilled at using these techniques may ignore the opportunity for deep listening as more traditional priorities like time constraints or following directions may dominate their mind. When this happens the opportunity to listen deeply may not even be a priority. But, without deeply listening to what students are saying, these techniques, which are meant to increase student voice and autonomy, are merely a protocol for increasing student "airtime" in the classroom.

While increasing student "airtime" has many benefits, including deepening learning, we need to pay extra attention to the kind of listening we do when we are facilitating collaborative and creative experiential learning. In academic classes, many of these techniques are used to give students a chance to use their voice and talk about content that is outside the realm of their personal life experiences. In facilitating social and emotional learning role-plays, the lives and experiences of our students are inextricable from the content of the lesson. Their voices and their ideas are inseparable from the content of their learning. So, we need to listen deeply and creatively in order to support them.

In social and emotional learning role-plays, we are asking students to take risks by sharing personally about emotions, conflicts, and problems they have experienced. We need to be emotionally and mentally available to support them in taking those risks. We are asking students to think creatively by proposing ideas for role-plays and solutions to the problems they explore as a class. We can't support them in that endeavor unless we listen deeply and respectfully to their ideas. We are asking them to practice social and emotional skills. We can't support them in deliberate practice unless we listen deeply to their first, second, and third attempts at skill practice and offer them useful feedback on how on to improve. And, we are asking them to collaborate and make group decisions. We can't do that unless we listen deeply to the relationships, connections, and contradictions between the ideas that arise within the group.

We often talk to students about active listening. We might tell them that their bodies should be still and their eyes should be focused on the speaker, that they might nod to show interest, and that they should not interrupt. Journalist and author Celeste Headlee makes an interesting point about these common active listening tips when she proposes in a TED Talk that "There is no reason to learn how to show you are paying attention if you are, in fact, paying attention." So, our students may perform the look of active listening, but if they are not mentally and emotionally engaged with what they are hearing, no real communication will occur. We know this is true when we ask students who appear to be listening a question and get a blank stare in response.

But, haven't we all learned to appear engaged while our hearts and minds are truly elsewhere? In certain environments this performed engagement may be considered polite behavior. We may have done this at our last family gathering, when our partner talked at length about their day, or when our boss rambled on about a future project, or we may have done this with our students. Yet, we all feel better when people actively listen to us. And, as teachers, we often want our students to actively listen to us and each other. But, how much do we actively listen to them?

Hearing is a physical function of the ears, but listening takes place in the heart and mind. There are many barriers to opening our hearts and minds to the process of deep listening. True listening involves the ability to set aside our own concerns and judgments and become deeply curious about the thoughts, feelings, and points of view of another. But, how do we set aside our own concerns, biases, and opinions to truly listen to our students deeply and creatively? What do we need to do internally so that we can allow ourselves to be influenced and inspired by their ideas as we facilitate social and emotional learning role-plays? Here are some tips:

- Don't multitask. Set your full attention on listening.
- Listen with the intent to understand and appreciate, rather than reply. Resist the urge to form responses in your mind, and put your attention on listening more.
- Assume that you will learn something by listening to your students and become curious.
- Resist the urge to reduce or simplify student thinking in your mind.
- Pay attention to and become curious about the details of each student's speech—the tone of voice, the pace of speaking, the word choice—and ask yourself what this tells you about their intended content.
- Listen with your body. Pay attention to the body language of the speaker and make note of the emotional undertones that their body expresses. Pay attention to how your body feels as you listen to them.
- Resist the urge to force your agenda.
- Be open to the idea that the conversion will end in an entirely unexpected place.
- Stay curious about student ideas even when you don't fully understand them.
- Interrupt your impulse to correct student ideas that you think are wrong and instead become curious about the basis of student thinking. Ask yourself why this student might be thinking what they are thinking and let the dialogue play out so that you can discover more.
- Challenge your own biases with intrapersonal (self-to-self) dialogue. When a student says something that you disagree with, ask

yourself why you are reacting so strongly. Identify your own biases and judgments and take responsibility for them.

- Challenge your need to control student expression. If students use language that you don't understand, ask yourself if you are biased against the use of words that may be unfamiliar to you. This is not to condone the use of hurtful language but to examine the role that culture plays in expression. For instance, if you do not understand Spanish but most of your students do, it may be perfectly appropriate for them to use some Spanish words to express themselves; if you do not allow this, you would be showing your own cultural bias for English only.

- Actively empathize with your students by making an effort to understand, without judgment, why they feel and think the way that they do. As they are sharing their feelings and thoughts about their position in the world and how it has impacted their experiences, emotions, and opinions, listen deeply and make an effort to understand their point of view emotionally and mentally.

FOLLOW STUDENT LEADS

If we make the efforts to relinquish control of dialogue and listen deeply to our students, we will be in a position to truly follow student leads and enhance the flow of student ideas. This is an exciting place to be as a teacher-facilitator. As we relinquish control and listen deeply to our students, we will begin to see more clearly the ideas that they are drawn to exploring.

We may discover that our students have moved their own discussion in a direction that is different from our expectations. We may discover that their point of view on an issue is something that we had neither thought of nor planned for. We may discover that they possess insights and knowledge of which we were previously unaware. We may discover that our plans for the discussion are inadequate and that their thinking has moved into a realm that we had not considered.

These are all exciting discoveries, as they point to the vibrancy of student voices and a deep engagement with student ideas.

If we have relinquished control and are deeply listening, and if we are committed to continuing in this approach, then we can powerfully follow student leads and help students make the most of their own discussions. This will not only help us to help our students develop their own ideas more fully, but it will also lead to us learning more deeply about our students and their unique perspectives.

The facilitation skills that have to do with following student leads hinge upon the foundational skills of relinquishing control and listening deeply. They involve paying attention to our own pacing, using our listening time within the discussion to track themes, and respectfully capturing these larger themes in summary statements and/or thematic questions that help students to develop their ideas further. Consider these facilitation techniques when working to follow student leads.

- Consciously allow the exchange between students to develop before contributing. Try to allow for at least six back-and-forth student exchanges to occur before offering any contribution of your own.
- Listen for key words and phrases that are shared by different group members. Ask yourself if these phrases might provide clues to identifying a theme for the discussion.
- Listen for similar ideas and make a mental or written note of them. Group them so that you can refer to them in a summary of the discussion.
- Listen for contradictory ideas and make a mental or written note of them. Ask yourself what the relationship between these ideas might be so that you can present this in a summary.
- Consider using hand gestures or simple note cards to suggest changes in direction in the group discussion. Use these yourself or allow students to use them. For instance:
  - A hand gesture or note card indicating "paraphrase"
  - A hand gesture or note card indicating "follow-up question"
  - A hand gesture or note card indicating "different opinion"
  - A hand gesture or note card indicating "expand upon your peers' thinking"
  - A hand gesture or note card indicating "alternate ending"
  - A hand gesture or note card indicating "change actors"
- Express appreciation and excitement for student ideas. Let your students know what you learned by listening to them and why you are excited and interested in the ideas they shared.
- Express empathy for the feelings and points of view that your students shared. Be specific. Name the experiences and feelings that your students voiced and describe how you shared in those feelings and thoughts, in your own way, as you listened.
- Summarize the flow of student ideas carefully and express admiration for what was shared.
- Summarize the flow of student ideas, both unified and contradictory, and ask higher-order thinking questions to push student thinking.
  - Prediction: What do you think will happen if _____?
  - Experimentation: There are many ways to _____. How would you like to approach _____?

- Comparison: Can you explain the differences and similarities between _____ and _____?
- Analysis: Now that we have taken time to explore _____, what are the benefits of using this communication technique in our real lives?
- Synthesis: How could we combine _____ and _____ to create an approach to this problem that might be even more useful?

- Ask creative questions that will help expand the role-plays, such as:

  - What effect would it have if _____?
  - What alternative ways can we think of to solve this problem?
  - If we changed _____, how would that affect the other characters?
  - I'm excited about what we just saw in this role-play, and I'd like to see this go further. How could this story continue?

In summary, many of the facilitation techniques that we already have as teachers are powerful, effective, and useful in facilitating social and emotional learning. All of our experience in using the distributive dialogue techniques that are now common in classrooms will come in handy when we are facilitating collaborative and creative experiential learning. But, we need to pay extra attention to relinquishing control, listening deeply, and following the flow of student ideas when we are using these techniques while facilitating social and emotional learning role-plays.

Unlike academic subjects where facilitation techniques often serve to give students a chance to engage in peer-to-peer dialogue before returning to more top-down and traditional instruction, social and emotional learning role-plays are a type of experiential learning where our students are learning by doing. We need to give them as much autonomy as possible, and we need to put our attention on listening to them and supporting their collaboration and creativity.

CONCLUSION

As we move into the second half of this book, which will delve into SEL role-play lessons, let's develop a shared vision of what our classrooms may look like as we engage our students in SEL role-plays. We know that in all our classrooms there will be an open area in the center of the room so that class members can easily hold eye contact. We know that all students will engage in kinetic and vocal warm-ups and participate in brainstorming ideas for role-plays. The group will share in the responsibilities of acting, observing behavior, offering suggestions to actors, trying different approaches to the problem presented in the role-play, and contributing to and controlling the flow of discussion. And, all students will engage in additional skills practice.

Teachers will act as teacher-facilitators using the many skills they already have to distribute dialogue and adding to them the ideas of relinquishing control, listening deeply, and following the flow of student ideas. And, they will encourage and support the deliberate practice of SEL skills by challenging students to step out of their comfort zones in their skills practice and offering as much one-on-one support as possible. Though we may not arrive at this shared vision on our first, second, or even third attempt at delivering an SEL classroom role-play lesson, we can keep it in mind as we and our students develop our skills.

FOUR

Social and Emotional Learning and Culturally Responsive Teaching

A BRIEF HISTORY OF SCHOOLS AND OPPRESSION (AND HOW SEL CAN HELP)

In simple terms, oppression involves the favoring of one social group over another by people, groups, or institutions that hold power. Oppression is maintained through social norms, stereotypes, biases, prejudices, discrimination, institutional rules, laws, and law enforcement.

The word "oppression" is a strong word and it has various meanings. When hearing the word, the first thing that comes to many people's minds is the description of authoritarian political regimes that directly deny their citizens basic rights. But there are a wide range of behaviors that could be considered examples of oppression. In general terms, oppression describes any situation where those in positions of power use bias, stereotypes, prejudice, discrimination, and other privileges of their position to deny rights, respect, and access to opportunity to those with less power.

In light of this broader definition, we must look at the fact that schools are powerful institutions and we, as teachers, represent the institutions for which we work. We hold tremendous power in our classrooms, and while it may be hard to face, we need to make sure that we are not consciously or unconsciously using our power to oppress our students. This is true for every school in every country on Earth, but it is especially true in the United States, which has always been a diverse country, and stands to grow in its diversity during the twenty-first century and beyond.

In particular, as teachers of social and emotional learning, which draws on the personal experiences of all our students, we need to make

53

sure that we are prepared to fully embrace and honor the diversity of personal experiences that our students bring into our classroom. If we doubt certain experiences shared by one student and elevate those of another, if we imply that there is a "normal" way to act and an "abnormal" way to act, if we value one student's way of expressing themselves and chastise another for their choice of words, we have put ourselves at odds with the spirit of the curriculum and have stepped into the waters of oppression. In social and emotional learning lessons, we are providing access to information that allows students to become more self-aware and better manage their relationships and problems; therefore, if we allow our own biases to prevent us from providing equal access to social and emotional learning opportunities, we are acting oppressively and misusing our power.

This is a hard fact to face, but it is one we need to consider. We may not intend to act oppressively, but we may do it nonetheless.

ACHIEVEMENT GAP OR TEACHING GAP?

Since the landmark 1954 Supreme Court decision in *Brown v. Board of Education*, in which the justices ruled unanimously that racial segregation of children in public schools was unconstitutional, our schools in the United States have been integrated in name. Yet, due to the impacts of oppression outside the school walls, such as redlining and discriminatory hiring practices, many of our public schools remain largely segregated. And, in schools that do have a diverse populations, there is ample evidence that though our students may have equal access to education they are not equally served by it.

The "achievement gap," as measured by student performance on standardized tests and college attendance, has long told us that, on average, students of color underperform in school as compared to their white peers. But, standardized tests often measure knowledge of literature, language, or concepts that reflect the dominant white culture. Yet, all students, including white students, are resistant to learning material that ignores or underrepresents their own cultures.

Why is it that the reading list for students of diverse backgrounds is often composed of work by white American or European authors? Why would we expect students to be motivated to spend inordinate amounts of time learning and thinking about stories, real or imagined, that do not reflect their own lives and histories? Thankfully, social and emotional learning content requires that we center the unique experiences of all of our students. But do we equally value the diversity of the experiences that are shared?

In addition, it is well known that students of color suffer harsher disciplinary consequences in school for the same disciplinary offenses as their white peers. A Government Accountability Office analysis of civil rights data collected by the Department of Education concluded that, in some cases, students of color may account for up to 34 percent of all school suspensions though students of color represent only 8 percent of the total school population.

In recent years, multiple African American students nationwide have been suspended for wearing dreadlocks. Can you imagine any white student being suspended for the style of their hair? Recently, two Native American high school students were asked questions by campus police while attempting to attend a tour at a public state college. Can we easily imagine a white student being summarily removed from a college tour for simply trying to participate in said tour?

These are two powerful examples of educational institutions oppressing students by denying them access to their right to an education. As teachers of social and emotional learning, if we worked for institutions that behaved in such a way, would we be willing to ally with these oppressed students? If we truly believed in honoring the unique experiences and emotional lives of all of our students, would we be willing to help these students apply social and emotional skills to manage the feelings, relationships, and problems that this oppression engendered within their own lives? These are challenging questions, but they are ones that deserve our time and attention.

APPLYING SEL TO THE CHALLENGES OF LIVING IN A DIVERSE SOCIETY

There is an intersection between social and emotional learning and culture. At that intersection lies the fact that many of the skills of social and emotional learning can be directly applied to help us deal with some of the most challenging social issues that we face in a diverse society, such as racial tension, class oppression, and cultural differences. But, this intersection can only become a working thoroughfare, where ideas flow easily and positively in all directions, if we as teachers of social and emotional learning have committed deeply to looking at our own biases and honoring the unique lives of all our students.

In a talk sponsored by the Society for Research in Child Development and given at the University of Virginia's Curry School of Education in the year following the descent of torch-carrying white supremacists on that campus, professor Joanna Lee Williams told the story of an African American tenth grade student asking her teacher, "How come the only thing we ever learn about black people is slavery?"

Williams pointed out that this question is valid, well observed, and likely came from years of waiting to learn about other aspects of her own culture aside from the oppression they suffered. She recounted sadly that this student's question was treated as defiance and disobedience and let the audience know that the student was asked to leave the class. The student was essentially oppressed, denied access to the education she sought, for asking why she can only learn about the oppression of her own people. Williams then wondered aloud if the question would have been treated as defiance if it was asked by a white student.

It is one thing to talk about the "achievement gap" and inequitable discipline policies in our schools on broad terms, and it is another thing to begin to really look at the specific conditions in the classroom that may cause or contribute to both. As teachers of social and emotional learning, we need to begin to think deeply about the classroom practices that contribute to lack of student engagement and biased disciplinary responses that may actually be targeting students not for their behavior but for their cultural expression. And, we need to be working, through our learning about and teaching of social and emotional skills, to help students and adults change both of these all too common problems.

What if, rather than talking about the "achievement gap" and looking at how to change student performance, we talked about the "teaching gap" and looked at how to change our pedagogy to better meet the needs of all our students? What if instead of examining the suspension rate, which tracks how often students of color are suspended, we looked at the inclusion rate, which might track how many invitations were made to all students to meaningfully engage and participate in academic and nonacademic activities in school, invitations that could be made through the culturally relevant delivery of a social and emotional learning program?

What if we looked at the oppressive tendencies within our schools and changed ourselves rather than looking at the effects of that oppression and blaming our students for their responses? And, most important for our work in social and emotional learning, what if we make time to examine our own biases and to ensure that we listen to, value, and include the voices and experiences of all of our students equitably?

CULTURALLY RELEVANT PEDAGOGY

> Teaching is about meeting the person you want to share information with on their own cultural terms. Where are they embedded? What are the examples that mean something to them? The educator has to be able to enter the learner's mind and be aware of how they view the world.
>
> —Christopher Emdin, award-winning author and science educator

Emdin is well known for using hip-hop to teach science and math in urban settings. His books *For White Folks Who Teach in the Hood* and *Urban Science Education for the Hip-Hop Generation* are both powerful testimonies to the skillful use of culturally relevant communication in the classroom.

By using hip-hop as a means of communication, he has inspired a genera-tion of teens to find their own voices in the sciences and has provided multiple examples of how to change the tone and style of a classroom so that it truly reflects the cultural style of its members. His is one powerful example of culturally relevant pedagogy.

Gloria Ladson-Billings originated the term "culturally relevant peda-gogy" and speaks about it in her book *The Dreamkeepers: Successful Teach-ers of African American Children*. In this book Ladson-Billings took an alter-nate approach to the well-known problems of achievement and engage-ment challenges and disciplinary issues between students of color and their teachers. Rather than looking at what students and teachers were doing wrong that might cause these problems, she decided to find teach-ers who had masterfully avoided these problems in their classrooms. She wanted to capture, analyze, and share these successes, these inspiring exceptions to the rule, with others educators. She essentially chose a strength-based rather than a deficit-based approach to finding solutions to these well-defined problems, and the concept of culturally relevant pedagogy is what emerged from her study.

At a 2017 talk at the Alliance for Catholic Education, Ladson-Billings distilled her approach to culturally relevant pedagogy under three main categories. She defined them as three equally weighted parts of an inte-grated pedagogical framework. She also made clear that, while her re-search has looked specifically at the successful education of students of color, these pedagogical practices will benefit all students, meaning stu-dents of all racial and ethnic backgrounds and abilities. In our teaching of social and emotional learning, which draws so directly from student lives and interests, it is important that we embrace these ideas. They are as follows:

1. Supporting learning and developing high expectations for all stu-dents
2. Developing cultural competency
3. Encouraging social, political, and critical consciousness

The first tenet may seem obvious. All educators, consciously at least, tend to want their students to do well. But, Ladson-Billings makes a powerful point about the tendency to develop our expectations in response to test-ing students on what we have actively delivered and our students have passively absorbed.

She proposes that we develop our expectations of our students in response to their active and personal engagement and demonstration of knowledge. She emphasizes a pedagogy that provides equal access to information and material for all students, active and personal involve-ment with the information and materials as part of the learning process, and higher-order thinking over rote learning. Emdin's work, in which he provides students with science concepts and facilitates their personal and active engagement with these concepts through the writing of hip-hop lyrics, is a great example of the kind of support for learning and high expectations that Ladson-Billings is talking about.

In order to do this we also need to look at our own biases and question whether we truly, as in the words of Emdin, are ready to meet people "on their own cultural terms." We need to ask ourselves if we have already decided who will do well and who will do poorly and therefore have already limited the access to materials and information based on these biases. We need to ask ourselves if we have already leveled children unconsciously or consciously in a manner that makes us lower our expectations for them and therefore engage them in rote rather than higher-order learning.

These are hard questions, but we need to wrestle with them if we truly want our teaching to be engaging for students from all cultural backgrounds and all learning styles. And, in the teaching of social and emotional learning, which centers the experience of all our students, we especially need to ask ourselves these questions. For, if we diminish a student's culture in the course of a social and emotional learning lesson, we will communicate that not only is their culture inferior, but so is their humanity.

"Developing cultural competency" refers to a teacher's knowledge of the cultural backgrounds of the students in their class. One of the misconceptions about cultural competency for teachers is the idea that the teacher must be fluent in the cultural practices of all the students in their classroom.

Some classrooms in the United States are quite diverse. I can think of one bilingual class I visited in Ditmas Park, Brooklyn, which is one of the most diverse neighborhoods in the country, if not the world, where the students spoke a total of fifty-three home languages. It was an incredible site to observe independent reading time where, in side-by-side stations with headphones, students silently read along to Haitian Creole books on tape, Wolof books on tape, Arabic books on tape, Spanish books on tape, and Polish books on tape. Clearly, it would be impossible for this teacher to demonstrate cultural fluency with all of the cultures represented in her class.

Ladson-Billings states that, at a basic level, developing cultural competency asks that teachers are fluent in the cultural practices of at least two cultures, their own and another that is widely represented in their class. In the simplest sense, any student who is not a member of the dominant white culture in the United State is themselves required to develop fluency in more than one culture for basic survival. And, this fluency in the cultural practices of more than one cultural group teaches everyone basic social and emotional skills of code-switching and empathy that will serve them throughout their lives.

So, in this light, Ladson-Billings's recommendation that teachers be fluent in the cultural practices of at least two cultures seems reasonable, especially knowing that every nonwhite and differently abled student is working to develop the same level of cultural fluently just by being who they are in a society that favors white, or European American, culture.

It is also important, when developing cultural fluency, to value diversity and become conscious of the dynamics inherent when cultures interact. All we need do is imagine ourselves in the role of the bilingual education teacher in Ditmas Park, Brooklyn. She valued and honored the diversity in her classroom and the culture of every student in the class, even if she did not have deep knowledge of their culture. She did this by learning some of the words and phrases from their native languages and by consciously building a bridge between their native languages and English through books on tapes, phrase and word translation walls, and conversation that incorporated words from English and their languages as a means of language acquisition.

Lastly, encouraging, social, political, and critical consciousness, as defined by Ladson-Billings, is a natural response to an American society that is full of social divisions based on class, race, ethic, religious, gender, and other categories. We must encourage all students to apply the knowledge that they learn in school to their unique and complicated lives outside of school. And we must push ourselves to ensure that our teaching makes the relevant connections between school and life.

The usefulness of education is essential not only for student engagement in school, but for student engagement in life. In this sense, Ladson-Billings suggests teachers actively help students to make connections between their community, national, and global identities. These values align perfectly with the core of social and emotional learning, which looks at how students can use social and emotional skills to manage the emotions, relationships, and conflicts in their own lives.

SEL AND CULTURE

When we speak about race, ethnicity, culture, diversity, and related topics on sociological terms, we tend to come up with broad and general definitions that we apply to larger, observable social patterns. These observations are useful in terms of understanding the world in which we live and how we tend to interact with one another on general terms.

Social and emotional learning as a discipline is different. While it attempts to find ways of addressing larger social problems, it often finds as its solutions skills that are embedded in psychological concepts. We could think of social and emotional learning as a discipline that looks to solve social and interactive problems through the use of applied psychology. The field of cognitive behavioral therapy, which is short-term therapy with a goal of changing patterns of thinking or behavior, shares much with skill-based social and emotional learning approaches such as the one presented in this book.

Social and emotional learning as a field has been criticized for ignoring issues of race, ethnicity, diversity, and culture, as has the broader field of psychology. The five social and emotional learning competencies of self-awareness, self-management, social awareness, relationship skills, and responsible decision-making do not specifically name issues around race, culture, and diversity directly, though many SEL programs attempt to address these issues. In most SEL curricula, this is done by grouping the lessons related to these issues into a separate unit—for instance, a "Diversity Unit." But, this approach of creating segregation and separation between the larger body of SEL knowledge and issues of race, ethnicity, culture, and diversity seems to mirror and justify some of the valid criticism of the field.

Because in the United States we live in a diverse society, we all experience, in different ways, the challenges and the richness that this diversity affords. Issues of race, ethnicity, culture, language, diversity, and related topics are part of our daily lives because they are part of daily life in the United States of America. So, they must be directly and consistently integrated, through the pedagogical style as well as the curricular materials, in any effective social and emotional learning program.

Howard C. Stevenson develops culturally relevant, in-the-moment, and strength-based measures, and therapeutic interventions that teach emotional and racial literacy. His work is a strong example that supports the idea that social and emotional learning can be directly useful in addressing issues of race, culture, diversity, and ethnicity in the United States. Trained as a clinical psychologist and researcher, he has developed a series of self-management interventions that can be practiced and performed by individuals when they are confronted with racially charged situations. These skills are drawn directly from social and emotional learning and involve emotional literacy, reading body language, self-talk, and mindful breathing.

Stevenson's work is a powerful example of the intersection between social and emotional learning and culture becoming that fully working thoroughfare where ideas flow easily and positively in all directions. He has identified key social and emotional learning skills that can be directly applied to help students deal with some of the most challenging incidents of racial tension in their own lives.

Issues of race, ethnicity, diversity, difference, culture, and related topics are so enmeshed in our everyday lives in the United States that they cannot be contained in a separate and segregated "unit" in a social and emotional learning curriculum. These issues impact us all deeply on a social and emotional level as we go about our lives in this country. For this reason, they need to be seamlessly woven into any effective SEL curriculum.

To this end, this curriculum includes a number of unique lessons under each competency that deal with issues of race, ethnicity, culture, diversity, and related topics. It also includes role-play suggestions — in the majority of the SEL lessons — that suggest an exploration of social and emotional issues that arise because of both the richness and the challenges of living in a diverse society. Meaning, even in lessons where the SEL skill being taught is not directly related to issues of race, ethnicity, difference diversity, or culture, there are suggestion of how students could apply the use of the SEL skill to a real-life situation that involved these issues. So, a teacher could touch on issues of culture and diversity in nearly every lesson they deliver, if they so choose.

CONCLUSION

This book is by no means attempting to catalog all of the complex ways that race, ethnicity, difference, diversity, and culture affect us in our lives in the United States. But, I do wish to include these issues definitively in the overall scope of SEL, and, in the spirit of the work of Howard C. Stevenson, I want to work to expand the way that SEL can directly help our students as they navigate these issues in their own lives.

In order to do that, we must acknowledge, in our pedagogy and our materials, how powerful and present these issues are for us all. Only by opening ourselves to the challenge of culturally responsive pedagogy, so eloquently detailed by Gloria Ladson-Billings, can we hope to truly reach all of our students in the teaching of SEL, or any other subject.

II

SEL Role-Plays for the Classroom

FIVE

Curriculum Organization

In chapter 1, we learned about the five SEL competencies identified by the Collaborative for Academic, Social, and Emotional Learning, or CASEL, a leading advocacy organization for social and emotional learning in our schools. The curricular section in this book will use the CASEL SEL competencies as an organizational understructure, while also incorporating an integrated approach to culturally relevant pedagogy.

SEL skills are grouped together under the five SEL competencies of self-awareness, self-management, social awareness, relationship skills, and responsible decision-making. In addition, each skill is identified in a themed track that allows for an alternate approach to ordering the material. These tracks include Listening to Our Bodies, Listening to Our Minds, Listening to Our Emotions, and Listening to Our Environment. Educators may move through the curriculum material one SEL competency at a time or one track at a time, or they may choose to customize a curriculum map based on the needs of their students. Culturally relevant pedagogy should be woven into any approach that an educator takes to the curriculum.

Figure 5.1 is an overview of the SEL competencies, SEL skills, and themed tracks. You may use this as a reference of all the SEL skills covered or to choose an organizational approach (by competency, by track, or customized) that best suits your needs.

ORGANIZING YOUR CURRICULAR APPROACH BY SEL COMPETENCY

If you choose to approach the curriculum through the organizational structure of the SEL competencies, there is a built-in scaffolding that can support this decision. While CASEL organizes these competencies on a

SEL COMPETANCIES					
TRACKS	**Self Awareness**	**Self Management**	**Social Awareness**	**Relationship Skills**	**Responsible Decision Making**
Listening to Our Bodies	Physical Sensations Identity and Assumptions	Deep Breathing and Meditation Identity, Skin Color, and Culture	Personal Space Nonverbal Communication	The Power of "No" Setting Personal Boundaries	Safe Ways to Be an Ally
Listening to Our Minds	Mindsets Metacognition	Self Talk and Shifting Mindsets Neutrality Persistence	Code Switching Cognitive Empathy	Thinking Time Do-Overs Paraphrasing	Identifying Underlying Causes Wants, Needs, Priorities
Listening to Our Emotions	Expanding Our Emotional Vocabulary	Understanding Anger Understanding Fear and Anxiety Understanding Sadness Coping Strategies for Anger, Fear, and Sadness	Rules and Norms Emotional Display Rules	Positive Affirmations Emotional Empathy I Feel Messages	Compassionate Empathy I Need Messages
Listening to Our Environment	Our Underlying Needs	Understanding Bias Understanding Stereotype	Understanding Prejudice Understanding Discrimination	Passive/Assertiveness/ Aggressive	Mediation Standing Up to Oppression
	CULTURALLY RELEVENT PEDAGOGY				

Figure 5.1.   Curriculum Framework

wheel, without favoring a particular order, we can logically organize them by moving from intrapersonal skills, or those communication skills that allow us to engage with our own mind and emotions, to interpersonal skills, which involve our communication with others. Looked at in this manner, the skills of self-awareness provide the basis for developing the skills of self-management, the skills of self-management provide the basis for developing the skills of social awareness, and the skills of social awareness provide the basis for developing relationships skills. The skills in all these competencies, collectively, provide the basis for responsible decision-making. With all this in mind, it can be useful to move through the curricular material in this order.

Self-Awareness

Self-awareness, as defined by CASEL, is "the ability to accurately recognize one's own emotions, thoughts, and values, and how they influence behavior." The core of this competency is the ability to recognize the physical, mental, and emotional components of our inner lives. In curricular terms, self-awareness can be understood as the skills that, if practiced regularly, will help us become aware of the content our inner life. These core skills are shown in fig. 5.2.

Self-Management

Self-management, as defined by CASEL, is "the ability to regulate one's emotions, thoughts, and behaviors in different situations." The core of this competency is the ability to wrestle with and regulate our inner physical, mental, and emotional lives in ways which are positive and productive. In curricular terms, self-management can be understood as the skills that, if practiced regularly, will help us to manage our bodies, thoughts, and feelings in positive and productive ways. These core skills are shown in fig. 5.3.

Social Awareness

Social awareness, as defined by CASEL, is "the ability to take the perspective of and empathize with others, including those from different backgrounds and cultures. The ability to understand social and ethical norms for behavior and to recognize family, schools, and community resources and support." The core of this competency is the ability to look outward to our community and interact with other members of our community in ways that are positive. In curricular terms, social awareness can be understood as the skills that, if practiced regularly, will help us form positive connections to the larger groups of which we are a part. These core skills are shown in fig. 5.4.

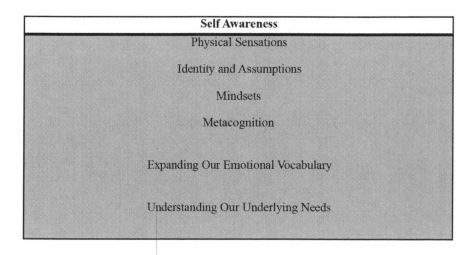

Figure 5.2. Self Awareness

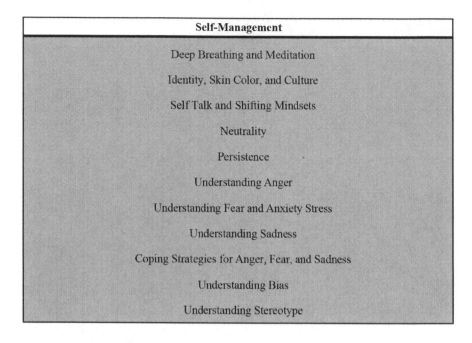

Self-Management
Deep Breathing and Meditation
Identity, Skin Color, and Culture
Self Talk and Shifting Mindsets
Neutrality
Persistence
Understanding Anger
Understanding Fear and Anxiety Stress
Understanding Sadness
Coping Strategies for Anger, Fear, and Sadness
Understanding Bias
Understanding Stereotype

Figure 5.3.   Self Management

Relationship Skills

Relationship skills, as defined by CASEL, are "the ability to establish and maintain healthy and rewarding relationships with diverse individuals and groups. The ability to communicate clearly, listen well, cooperate with others, resist inappropriate social pressure, negotiate conflict constructively, and seek and offer help when needed." The core of this competency is maintaining connections with others through meaningful, one-on-one interactions and ongoing relationships. In curricular terms, relationship skills can be understood as the skills that, if practiced regularly, will help us form long-lasting and positive one-on-one relationships with others. These core skills are shown in fig. 5.5.

Responsible Decision-Making

Responsible decision-making, as defined by CASEL, is "the ability to make constructive choices about personal behavior and social interactions based on ethical standards, safety concerns, and social norms. The realistic evaluation of consequences of various actions and consideration of the well-being of oneself and others." The core of this competency is the ability to weigh options and make choices in a productive manner. In curricular terms, responsible decision-making can be understood as the

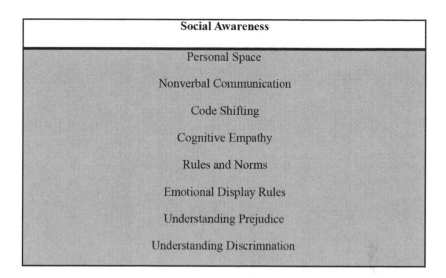

Figure 5.4. Social Awareness

skills that, if practiced regularly, will help us make choices that are beneficial to ourselves and to others. These core skills are shown in fig. 5.6.

ORGANIZING YOUR CURRICULAR APPROACH BY TRACK

Alternatively, each SEL competency includes skills that span a wide range of learning styles. It may be helpful to follow tracks designed to bolster each of these learning styles as they move across all five SEL competencies. With this in mind, this book also groups the SEL skills menu by the tracks: Listening to Our Bodies, Listening to Our Minds, Listening to Our Emotions, and Listening to Our Environment. By following these tracks, you will build and deepen a set of related skills in each learning style, and students may have the chance to develop a greater comfort with each learning style. This approach may be more suited to your students and their learning styles, your teaching style, and the issues that arise in your classroom.

Listening to Our Bodies

In Listening to Our Bodies, the focus is on the physical or kinetic modality of learning. All the SEL skills in this track involve an awareness of, or engagement with, one's own physical life or the physical life of others. In curricular terms, the Listening to Our Bodies track can be understood as the skills that, if practiced regularly, will help use our

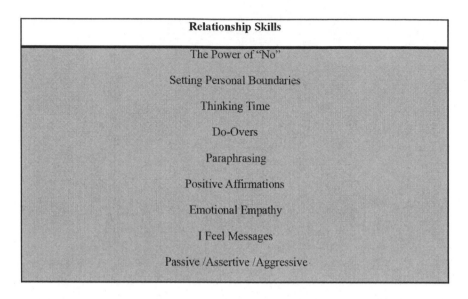

Relationship Skills
The Power of "No"
Setting Personal Boundaries
Thinking Time
Do-Overs
Paraphrasing
Positive Affirmations
Emotional Empathy
I Feel Messages
Passive /Assertive /Aggressive

Figure 5.5. Relationship Skills

physical awareness and mastery to execute choices that improve our relationship with ourselves and others (fig. 5.7).

Listening to Our Minds

In Listening to Our Minds, we focus on gaining and practicing cognitive skills that support our social and emotional life. All SEL skills in this track focus on the ways in which we can observe, engage with, and change our own thinking in relationship to ourselves and others. In curricular terms, the Listening to Our Minds track can be understood as the skills that, if practiced regularly, will allow us to observe and adjust our thinking and improve our relationship with ourselves and others (fig. 5.8).

Listening to Our Emotions

In Listening to Our Emotions, we focus on articulating and understanding our emotional life. All SEL skills in this track focus on the ways in which we can experience and communicate emotions in relationship to ourselves and others. In curricular terms, the Listening to Our Emotions track can be understood as the skills that, if practiced regularly, will allow us to observe, experience, communicate, and shift our emotions and improve our relationship with ourselves and others (fig. 5.9).

Responsible Decision-Making
Safe Ways to be an Ally
Identifying Underlying Causes
Wants, Needs, Priorities
Compassionate Empathy
I Need Messages
Mediation
Standing Up to Oppression

Figure 5.6. Responsible Decisionmaking

Listening to Our Environment

In Listening to Our Environment, we focus on understanding and responding positively to our social environment. All SEL skills in this track focus on the ways in which we can observe, understand, and interact with our environment. In curricular terms, the Listening to Our Environment track can be understood as the skills that, if practiced regularly, will allow us to make a positive impact in our larger environment (fig. 5.10).

CUSTOMIZING YOUR CURRICULAR APPROACH

There is some overlap between the skills presented under all SEL competencies and tracks. There is no one "right way" to move through this material. And, sometimes the best way to move through any curriculum is by responding to the needs and interests of our students. It is possible to create, with your students in mind, a responsive curricula map that moves through this material in a way that best addresses their needs.

LESSONS

Each SEL skill lesson will be clearly identified at the top by SEL skill name, SEL competency, and track. A simple definition for the SEL skill will be provided in addition to a more detailed description so that teachers can present conceptual information as a basis for student discussion.

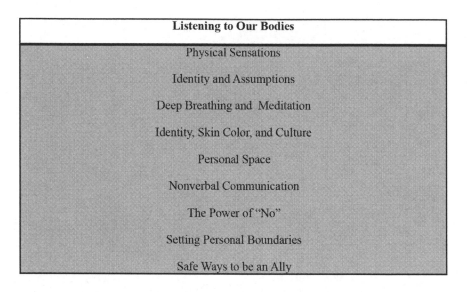

Figure 5.7. Listening to Our Bodies

Additional information is organized in line with chapter 2 steps and procedures and includes:

- **Kinetic Awareness** and **Vocal Warm-Up** suggestions
- Open-ended **Conversation Starter Questions** to help students identify their own experiences and come up with their own role-play ideas
- **Role-Play Ideas** to start off your class if students are shy about sharing their own role-play ideas or to supplement the ideas that they already shared
- **Freeze** and **Refine, Revise, Redo** ideas to help expand upon the discussion and the role-play itself
- **Everybody Practice** follow-up role-play practice in which all students can participate and refine their SEL skills
- **Wrapping It Up** synthesis questions

The facilitation strategies suggested in chapter 3 and the integration of culturally relevant pedagogy, as described in chapter 4, are always good to keep in mind. While it may take time to develop comfort with the format of these lessons, eventually you should feel comfortable relinquishing control, listening deeply, following the flow of student ideas, and watching and learning with your students as they practice the acquisition of new SEL skills.

Social and emotional learning is a lifelong process for everyone. The concepts and skills explored here are basic and foundational, but we all could likely use practice with them, even in adulthood. Although there is

Listening to Our Minds
Mindsets
Metacognition
Self Talk and Shifting Mindsets Neutrality
Persistence
Code Switching
Cognitive Empathy
Thinking Time
Do Overs
Paraphrasing
Identifying Underlying Causes
Wants, Needs, Priorities

Figure 5.8.   Listening to Our Minds

one lesson for each skill, it is unrealistic to think that anyone could master these skills in one lesson. Therefore, the lessons are meant to give you a starting point and a clear basis for exploration of each concept.

It is my hope that you will expand your own exploration of each concept and skill with additional role-plays created by you and/or students. None of these social and emotional skills can be fully absorbed without adequate practice, so staying on one concept for two or three sessions is optimal. In this sense, the lessons presented here are models to introduce you and your students to a concert or skill. But, using your own role-play ideas in additional sessions to continue the student practice is the purpose and is essential to developing these skills. Role-plays provide opportunities for practice, and the more practice the better!

I hope that you enjoy the process of learning with your students as you all acquire new SEL skills through the process of role-plays. Let's get started!

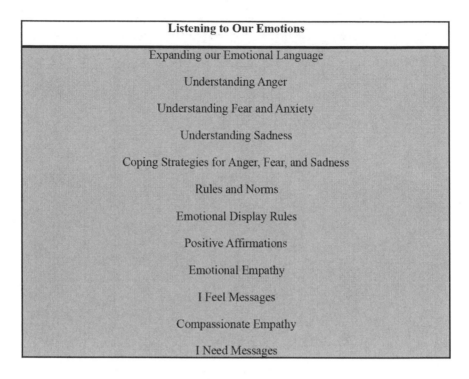

Figure 5.9.   Listening to Our Emotions

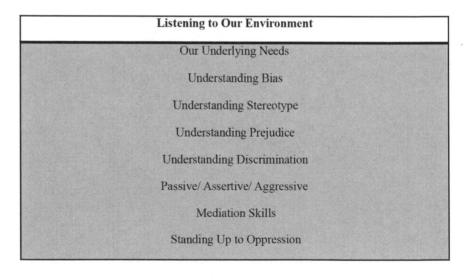

Figure 5.10.   Listening to Our Environment

SIX

The Lessons

PHYSICAL SENSATIONS

Competency: Self-Awareness

Track: Listening to Our Bodies

Definition: A physical sensation is a physical feeling resulting from something that happens to or within the body.

Detailed Description: We all experience physical sensations throughout the day. We might be cold, hungry, or sleepy. Based on these sensations, we decide how to get our needs met. If we are cold, we may throw on a sweater; if we are hungry, we may grab a snack; if we are sleepy, we rest. But, we also experience physical sensations that are connected to our emotions and thought processes. Expressions like "I have a lump in my throat," "I have butterflies in my stomach," "I froze," "My mind is racing," and "I was dragging myself" describe physical sensations that are associated with emotions and thought processes.

Kinetic Warm-Up: Play *Tense and Release*. Ask students to close their eyes and sit in a relaxed state. Ask them to tense their leg muscles for five seconds and then release them. Lead them through a cycle of legs, arms, torso, neck, and head before instructing them to open their eyes.

Vocal Warm-Up: In partners, have students improvise a conversation using one of the metaphorical phrases from the detailed description.

Conversation Starter Questions:

- What emotions do you think you might be feeling if you said, [*insert one of the phrases from detailed description*]?

- Can you describe a time you noticed your body changing based on the emotions you were experiencing?
- How does your body change when you are [*insert feeling word*]?

Role-Play Ideas: One character uses a phrase that describes their physical sensation. Their role-play partner asks, "What happened and what are you thinking or feeling right now?" The two characters explore the connection between physical sensations, thoughts, and feelings. Two characters use two different phrases, each drawing from their own cultural background, to explain the same feeling. The two characters help each other understand the meaning of their cultural expression and how two different expressions can mean the same thing.

Freeze Ideas: Explore the answer to the question "What are you thinking or feeling right now?" Explore the physical shape of the actor's body and how it conveys the thoughts and feelings their character described.

Refine, Revise, Redo: Actors change roles. Then, redo with another actor and another physical sensation.

Everybody Practice: Allow all class members to enact either of these role-plays in pairs from their seats, or in individual playing areas across the room.

Wrapping It Up—Synthesis Questions:

- What can the physical sensations in our bodies tell us about our own emotions and thoughts?
- Why might it be important to pay attention to the physical sensations in our bodies?
- How does our cultural background influence the way we express our emotions and physical sensations to others?

IDENTITY AND ASSUMPTIONS

Competency: Self-Awareness

Track: Listening to Our Bodies

Definition: Our personal identity is how we think about and define who we are to ourselves and others. It could include our roles in society, our talents and interests, our cultural or religious background, our ethnic or racial background, our political views, our gender or sexuality, and/or our physical attributes.

Detailed Description: We all have personal identities that could be called intersectional, meaning they describe various parts of ourselves. For instance, someone might identify themselves as an Iranian and African American, a political activist, and an actress (Yara Shahidi). Someone might say that they are an African American, an advanced math wizard, and a professional football player (John C. Urschel). Someone might say they are Southern, gay, an animal activist, and a talk show host (Ellen DeGeneres). Someone else might identify themselves as a Jewish American, a gymnast, and an abuse survivor (Aly Raisman). Someone else might say they are a Taiwanese American, a Christian, and an NBA player who graduated from Harvard (Jeremy Lin).

We all have various sides of us that help us understand who we are and how to describe ourselves to others. Our identities can be a source of pride or they can be something that we hide from others. However we feel about our own identities, it is common that people make assumptions about our identities based on how we appear to them.

Kinetic Warm-Up: Play *Identity Shuffle*. Invite students to stand in a circle. Share the sentence starter, "If you like to ____, find a new spot in the circle." Let one student finish the sentence by filling in whatever interests them. Whoever shares the same interest will shuffle and find a new spot in the circle. Repeat so that multiple students get a chance to take the lead.

Vocal Warm-Up: Invite students to sit in pairs and begin to explore their own intersectional identities by sharing with one another their roles in the family, their interests outside of school, their skills or talents, their cultural or ethnic background, and their political views if they have any. A student answer to this exercise might be something like, "I am a Puerto Rican older sister who loves science and works as a babysitter." Invite students back to the large circle to share their intersectional identities.

Conversation Starter Questions: We all have sides of ourselves that we feel proud of and sides of ourselves that we may hide. And, we all have been mistaken for being something we are not based on how we appear to other people.

- What part of your identity would people never know from looking at you?
- What do people assume about you based on how you appear to them?

Role-Play Ideas: Invite two students to improvise a scene between a female character who dresses in a more masculine manner and is often mistaken for a boy, and a male character who is new in the school and trying to make friends. He might say things like, "Where do the boys hang out at recess?" or "Where is the boy's bathroom?" or "Don't you hate it when girls are in your table group?"

Freeze Ideas: Freeze the scene right after the female character realizes that she is being misidentified as a boy.

- What might she be thinking and feeling?
- How do you feel when you are misidentified by others?
- How might she handle this situation?

Get suggestions from the audience, pick one, and allow the scene to play out.

Revise, Refine, Redo: Try another scenario where someone is misidentified due to the way they appear to others. For instance, a Spanish-speaking Latin American character assumes a Filipino character with a Spanish last name speaks his/her language; a white character, with little knowledge of Asian cultures, assumes that a Korean character is actually Chinese; an African American character assumes that his/her classmate identifies as black when they are biracial.

Everybody Practice: Have students speak in pairs about times where aspects of their own identities were misidentified by others. Ask them to discuss how this made them feel and how they responded to it at the time.

Wrapping It Up—Synthesis Questions: We all have intersectional identities. These identities change; the way we identify ourselves today may not be the way we identify ourselves in the future. And, others will always make assumptions about our identities based on the way we appear to them.

- What can we do to proudly embrace all aspects of who we are?
- What can we say to people who misidentify us based on their own assumptions and experiences?

MINDSETS

Competency: Self-Awareness

Track: Listening to Our Minds

Definition: A mindset is a habitual attitude that we hold about what is happening to us and around us.

Detailed Description: There is a common phrase, "Attitude is everything." We all shape our interpretation of what is happening to us and around us with our attitudes. A positive attitude encourages us to see the possibilities. A negative attitude makes everything seem problematic. We might express negative attitudes with the following statements:

- I will never be able to change this!
- I'd rather not even try!
- They are out to get me!
- If I don't _____, my whole life will be ruined.

Positive attitudes might be expressed with the following statements:

- If I put some effort into this, it will get better.
- I'm not sure what is on their minds.
- My whole life is not dependent on any one person or situation.

When our mindset is habitually negative, we call it a "fixed mindset" because it tends to make us focus on real or imagined problems. When it is positive, we call it a "growth mindset" because it allows us to focus on possibilities. Our mindset is our choice. And, a growth mindset will make us happier and make our lives much more fulfilling.

Kinetic Warm-Up: Play *Shake it Off!* As this lesson is about learning to shake off negative mindsets and attitudes, invite students to stand and gently shake out the tension they have in their bodies.

Vocal Warm-Up: Ask students to pair up and share negative mindsets or attitudes, where people focus on problems and limitations, that they have expressed themselves or heard expressed at school or at home.

Conversation Starter Questions:

- Can you remember a time when you had a negative idea that turned out to be false?
- Can you think of a time when your positive attitude helped to make a difficult situation easier to handle?
- What might happen if you think about a test and say to yourself, "I'll probably fail"? What if you say to yourself, "What can I do to prepare myself?"

Role-Play Ideas: Introduce the fixed mindset phrase "If I don't [*pass this test/learn to speak better English/make friends with the cool kids/lose weight/get an after-school job*], my whole life is ruined." Ask students to come up with a scenario where one character uses this phrase and the other convinces him/her to adopt a growth mindset by seeing possibilities instead of problems.

Freeze Ideas: Ask the class to share positive ways that the character can look at their situation.

Revise, Refine, Redo: Ask the actors to switch roles. Invite two new actors try out the role-play with a different situation triggering the use of this phrase.

Everybody Practice: Ask students to think of a situation in their lives where they might think, "I will never be able to change this!" In partners, ask them to help one another think of phrases that would promote a growth mindset in relation to the problem by searching for possibilities instead of problems.

Wrapping It Up—Synthesis Questions:

- What is the key difference between growth and fixed mindsets?
- Why might a growth mindset be important as you move through life?
- Who can you ask to help you develop a growth mindset when you are stuck in a fixed mindset?

METACOGNITION

Competency: Self-Awareness

Track: Listening to Our Minds

Definition: Metacognition is the ability to observe and analyze your own thinking process.

Detailed Description: Sometimes shifting from a fixed mindset to a growth mindset is easier said than done. But, if we are able to observe and analyze our own thinking, which is called metacognition, then we can choose to change it.

Kinetic Warm-Up: Play *Shift and Change*. As this lesson is about shifting stubborn thinking patterns, invite students to join you in standing and gently shifting their weight from one leg to the other. Then shift from standing to sitting and back again. Repeat this cycle three times.

Vocal Warm-Up: Ask students to work in small groups or pairs and respond to the prompt, "The best way to [*peel an onion/pass a soccer ball/ take a guitar solo/ask your parents for permission/get dressed in the morning/ talk to the police*] is _____." Encourage the group members to ask the speaker, "Why is this the best way to _____?" If we explain our own thinking and why we think what we do, we are practicing metacognition, even if we are talking about peeling an onion!

Conversation Starter Questions:

- Can you remember a time when you felt very stubborn and did not want to change your opinion about a situation? Why were you so stubborn?
- Can you think of a time when you were more flexible and did change your opinion? Why were you willing to be more flexible?

Role-Play Ideas: Metacognition is about explaining our thinking and examining why we think the way we do. Invite one student into the playing area. Present this student with the statement "Boys and girls can be best friends without any complications" and ask them to explain why they agree, disagree, or are unsure. Ask another student with a different idea into the playing area to share their thinking. Ask the two students to ask each other, "What in your experience made you come to this conclusion?" and "Are you open to changing your mind?"

Freeze Ideas: Invite the class to question their peers about their thinking on this same issue. This could be done in pairs or through direct questions to the players in the circle.

Revise, Refine, Redo: Invite other students into the playing area to respond to the statement "All human beings are created equal" or "If you are in trouble, the best thing to do is call the police."

Everybody Practice: In pairs, ask students to improvise a conversation where one character shares, "If I fail, everyone will laugh at me." The other character will ask them why they believe this is true and encourage them to shift from a fixed to a growth mindset by discussing other ways of thinking about failing.

Wrapping It Up—Synthesis Questions:

- Why might it be important to be able to explain your own thinking to others?
- Why might it be beneficial to stay flexible in your own thinking?

EXPANDING OUR EMOTIONAL VOCABULARY

Competency: Self-Awareness

Track: Listening to Our Emotions

Definition: We all experience a range of emotions throughout the day, but we often are at a loss as to how to best describe them. Expanding our emotional vocabulary can help.

Detailed Description: We all experience a set of basic emotions. There are differences of opinion about what these basic emotions are, but most people agree on these six: sadness, joy, fear, surprise, anger, and love. We also experience a wide range of related emotions, which have slight variations in meaning. But, because our emotional language is often limited, we may end up using the basic emotions to describe them. So, in order to better understand ourselves and be better understood by others, it is worth it to work on expanding our emotional vocabulary.

Kinetic Warm-Up: Play *Emotional Pictures*. Since this lesson is all about expanding emotional vocabulary, lead students in a series of prompts that follow this format: "How would you be sitting if you were [*sad/joyful/fearful/surprised/angry/feeling loved*]?" Encourage students to shift their bodies and faces to reflect these emotions.

Vocal Warm-Up: Working in pairs, ask students to improvise a sentence someone might say if they were feeling sad, joyful, fearful, surprised, angry, or loved that **does not** include any of these words. Encourage them to improvise in a vocal tone that reflects the emotion. For example, if someone was surprised, they might say, "I can't believe this is happening to me!"

Conversation Starter Questions:

- Can you describe a time when you were at a loss when trying to explain how you were feeling?
- Can you describe a time you listened to someone explain what they were feeling but did not understand them?
- Why might it be important to expand our emotional vocabulary?

Role-Play Ideas: Remind student of the basic emotions of sadness, joy, fear, surprise, anger, and love. Start with any one and invite students to enter the playing area if they have an approximate synonym, meaning a word that has a related but slightly different meaning. Ask them to share the word and their definition, then ask them to call on another student to replace them and do the same. For instance, for *sad* a student might say,

"Disappointed: when you are sad you did not get something you wanted." Ask other students to chart answers.

Freeze Ideas: Allow students to expand upon the definitions being shared by their peers.

Refine, Refine, Redo: Repeat for each of the basic emotions with the goal of generating at least ten approximate synonyms and definitions per emotion word.

Everybody Practice: Invite students to improvise a conversation in pairs where they use at least three words from the list generated that they have never used before in conversation.

Wrapping It Up—Synthesis Question:

- How will our conversations change if we commit to using more precise emotional vocabulary?

OUR UNDERLYING NEEDS

Competency: Self-Awareness

Track: Listening to Our Environment

Definition: We all have basic needs that relate specifically to our emotional health. If these basic needs are not met, we experience difficult emotions.

Detailed Description: There are different opinions about our basic needs as they relate to emotional health, but most people agree on these five basic needs: *safety*, or the assurance that our bodies and feelings will not be hurt; *security*, or the assurance that what we have (relationships, opportunities, objects) will not be taken from us; *belonging*, or a sense that we are welcomed into the groups of which we are a part; *respect*, the sense that people will listen to and consider our ideas; and *love*, or the sense that there is at least one person in our lives who loves us deeply. Part of self-care is understanding these basic needs and how we make sure that they are met in our own lives and the lives of others.

Kinetic Warm-Up: Play *Tableaus*. Divide students into five groups and assign each one of the five basic needs. Invite students to discuss the definition and create a tableau that expresses it.

Vocal Warm-Up: In the same groups, ask students to improvise conversations where one character fulfills another's basic need. The *belonging* group might share, "I'm excited that we are in the same group," and the *security* group might share, "I'll watch your bag for you."

Conversation Starter Questions:
When someone threatens our basic needs, we usually experience strong emotions.

- What do you experience when someone threatens [*your physical or emotional safety/to take away something you care about/to exclude you from a group*] or refuses [*to listen to consider your ideas/to honor your requests*] or acts [*like they don't love you/like you don't belong*]?

Role-Play Ideas: Using the conversation starters listed above, invite students to come up with a simple scenario in which someone's basic needs for safety, security, belonging, respect, or love are threatened. It is useful to do at least one scenario for each basic need so that the definitions become clear for your students. This lesson may be stretched out over more than one session so that all basic needs can be fully explored. Scenario ideas:

- *Safety*: A student comes into the school after witnessing a fight outside the school and is not sure what to do to keep herself safe.
- *Security*: A student notices his book bag has gone missing.
- *Belonging*: A student is excluded from a social group because of her cultural background.
- *Respect*: One student insults another student's work.
- *Love*: A student has just found out that his grandparents, who he is emotionally close to, are moving away.

Freeze Ideas: When one character's needs are threatened, call "freeze."

- What can you read on the face and body of this actor?
- What emotions might the character be experiencing?

Refine, Revise, Redo: Replay each scenario so that someone decides to listen to the character's unmet needs and tries to meet them by talking and/or trying to help directly solve the problem. Ask students to observe the differences between meeting another's needs and threatening another's needs.

Everybody Practice: In pairs, ask students to improvise a conversation where one character attempts to express their own needs and the other character attempts to meet them in some way. Reverse roles and repeat.

Wrapping It Up—Synthesis Questions:
We are responsible for getting our own basic needs met, but we are also responsible for helping others to make sure their basic needs are met.

- What can we do to make sure the basic needs of others are met?
- What can we do to make sure our basic needs are met?

DEEP BREATHING AND MEDITATION

Competency: Self-Management

Track: Listening to Our Bodies

Definition: Deep breathing and meditation constitute a process by which we calm our thoughts and quiet our minds.

Detailed Description: Meditation is a method for calming the body and mind that has been in use for thousands of years. It is embedded in various religious traditions such as Buddhism, but is also practiced by all kinds of nonreligious people. One of the simplest ways to calm the mind is by closing our eyes, calming our bodies, and counting our breaths.

Kinetic Warm-Up: Play *Inhale/Exhale*. Invite your students to sit with their eyes closed. Gently lead them in a series of slow, deep breaths by counting the inhale and the exhale on a count of three. For example, "Inhale 1, 2, 3. Exhale 1, 2, 3. ONE. Inhale 1, 2, 3. Exhale 1, 2, 3. TWO." Repeat for ten cycles.

Vocal Warm-Up: Invite students to talk in pairs about how they feel after practicing deep breathing and what, if anything, occupied their minds.

Conversation Starter Questions:
Meditating helps us to become aware of our "busy minds," or the part of our mind that is occupied or distracted. Everyone's mind is different.

- When your mind is busy or distracted, with what is it occupied?
- When we mediate we are in dialogue with ourselves. What do you think this might mean?

Role-Play Ideas: One technique for meditating is to restart the counting of our breath at "one" each time our "busy mind" interrupts our "meditating/counting mind." Invite two students into the playing area. They will sit or stand and use only their voices for this role-play. One student will be the voice of the "busy mind" and the other student will be the voice of the "meditating/counting mind."

The "meditating/counting mind" will start taking deep breaths and counting aloud, as in the kinetic warm-up. The "busy mind" will interrupt by voicing thoughts, worries, interests, or dreams about the future. Each time it does, the "mediating/counting mind" character will begin again at "one."

Freeze Ideas: This is a role-play that demonstrates how we are in dialogue with ourselves as we meditate.

- What might the "meditating/counting mind" do to encourage the "busy mind" to calm down?
- What might the "busy mind" do to try to reduce the distractions?

Revise, Refine, Redo: Allow other students to voice the "meditating/counting mind" and the "busy mind" characters. Encourage groups to notice all the different types of thoughts that can occupy our minds.

Everybody Practice: Allow students to do this same role-play in pairs, alternating the roles of "busy mind" and "meditating/counting mind." Encourage them to voice their own thoughts when playing the "busy mind" character.

Wrapping It Up—Synthesis Question:

- How and when might it be helpful to meditate in our own lives?

IDENTITY, SKIN COLOR, AND CULTURE

Competency: Self-Management

Track: Listening to Our Bodies

Definition: Our personal identity is how we think about and define who we are to ourselves and others. It could include our roles in society, our talents and interests, our cultural or religious background, our ethnic or racial background, our political views, our gender or sexuality, and/or our physical attributes.

Detailed Description: We all have personal identities that could be called intersectional, meaning they describe various parts of ourselves. We all have various sides of us that help us understand who we are and help us describe ourselves to others. As we grow and change we may describe ourselves differently. Our skin color, or race, should we choose to use that term, is one part of our identity. The biological concept of race, which says that the human population of Earth can be divided into separate and distinct "races" based on various physical characteristics such as skin color or eye shape, has long been proven to be false.

In the truest biological sense, we are all equally and beautifully human, but the concept of race had great power as the world was colonized. Though it holds no true meaning in the biological sense, race is used as a way to categorize people into social groups based on how they look. As a result, we have created cultures that are associated with these groupings that we embrace and celebrate and use a way to further identify who we are. These color and cultural groupings have also been used to separate us through privilege, prejudice, discrimination, and oppression.

Though our skin color, or our race, if we choose to use that language, is only one part of our identity, it is a powerful part. This is especially true in the United States, where a very diverse citizenry comprises people of many different colors and cultures.

Kinetic Warm-Up: Play *Dance Party*. Using a digital music source, invite students to DJ a mini dance party where they play and dance to music that represents a wide variety of cultures within the citizenry of the United States.

Vocal Warm-Up: Invite students to sit in small groups and use the sentence starter "In my culture we like to _____."

Conversation Starter Questions: Culture, which can be simply defined as a set of agreements that a group of people shares, encompasses all kinds of practices, from the language people speak to the music they listen to, the foods they eat, and the type of humor they share. Sometimes we use ethnic words to describe culture. For instance, we might refer to

Asian culture or Middle Eastern culture. Other times, we use color words to talk about culture. For instance, we might refer to white culture, black culture, or brown culture.

- In what way does your skin color help you to connect with or understand your culture?
- In what way does your skin color prevent you from connecting with or understanding cultures that are different than yours?

Role-Play Ideas: Invite two students to improvise a conversation between friends about the fact that their parents don't mind who they hang out with now, but have told them that they don't want them to marry someone with a different skin color than theirs.

Freeze Ideas: Freeze the scene when the two characters are trying to decide if they agree with their parents.

- Are the parents really concerned about skin color or are they concerned about differences in culture?
- Do you think the parents' fears or concerns are valid?

Revise, Refine, Redo: Improvise a scene where group of kids is celebrating or practicing elements of their culture and teaching it to others who do not know about it. For instance, you might role-play Dominican kids dancing salsa, Chinese kids speaking Mandarin, or white kids practicing classical music.

Improvise a scene where an African American character is talking to a friend who says they are not dark enough to be black. Explore how this idea—that only a certain skin color will allow you to participate in a culture—can be very hurtful.

Everybody Practice: Invite students to work in pairs and answer these questions: What is one thing you love about your skin color? What is one thing your love about your culture?

Wrapping It Up—Synthesis Questions:
We all have personal identities that could be called intersectional, meaning they describe various parts of ourselves. Our skin color has a profound influence on our identity because skin color has been used to construct the concept of race. The concept of race is often used to describe aspects of culture.

- How do you think your skin color is related to your culture?
- In what ways does your culture encompass more than your skin color?

SELF-TALK AND SHIFTING MINDSETS

Competency: Self-Management

Track: Listening to Our Minds

Definition: Self-talk is the unspoken, inner monologue that influences our mindset.

Detailed Description: With practice, we can learn to become aware of our self-talk and shift it to positively affect our mindset and our mood.

Kinetic Warm-Up: Play *Eavesdropping on Myself.* Invite your students to sit with their eyes closed. Instead of counting deep breaths and calming their "busy minds," they will simply breathe slowly, at their own pace, and *observe* their "busy minds." Invite them to notice the self-talk in their minds as they sit in silence.

Vocal Warm-Up: Invite students to talk in pairs about the self-talk they just observed.

Conversation Starter Questions: Sometimes our "busy minds" are occupied with self-talk that is not very helpful. For example:

Judging: Thinking we or other people are not good enough
Mind reading: Thinking we know what other people are thinking
Magnifying: Thinking that something terrible will happen

- Do you recognize any of these thinking patterns from your observation of your "busy mind"?
- What emotions do you experience when your mind is busy with negative thought patterns?

Role-Play Ideas: Invite students into the playing area to role-play these situations.

- One student looks for a spot to sit in the lunchroom. The other students say, "We don't have any room for you."
- A student failed their math test, even though they love math and usually do well.

Freeze Ideas: Ask the class to identify the type of negative thinking—*judging, mind reading,* or *magnifying*—that each character might be experiencing and how they could shift it. For example:

- Role-Play 1: "No one likes me" (*mind reading*) might shift to "There are lots of kids to sit with in the lunchroom."

- Role-Play 2: "Now I'll never get into college" (*magnifying*) might shift to "I'm going to see if Malcolm, who did really well on this test, can explain how he got his answers."

Revise, Refine, Redo: Now that some positive self-talk ideas have been generated, replay each scenario and observe how the behaviors of all the characters shift when they practice positive self-talk. Positive self-talk changes not only our mindset and our mood, but also our behavior.

Everybody Practice: Practice shifting these negative self-talk statements to positive self-talk in pairs.

Judging: "That kid is such a loser. I don't want to be seen with him."
Mind reading: "I know my mom likes my sibling better than me."
Magnifying: "If I don't do well on this test, I'll get left back!"

Wrapping It Up—Synthesis Questions:

- Why might it be important to shift out of *judging, mind reading,* and *magnifying* and into more positive types of self-talk?
- How does positive self-talk change our behavior?

NEUTRALITY

Competency: Self-Management

Track: Listening to Our Minds

Definition: Neutrality is state of mind in which we refuse to take sides in an argument that does not involve us.

Detailed Description: When other people have an argument or disagreement, they may pressure us to take their side against someone else. This happens in families, in friendships, and at work. There are many reasons why taking sides could be harmful to us and the people involved. When we are not involved in the conflict we likely will not know what really happened, and we might damage our relationships with either person if we take sides. Unfortunately, the negative thinking patterns of *judgment, mind reading,* and *magnifying* can make it hard to be neutral, so it is important that we learn how to shift our thinking and remain neutral when others push us to take sides.

Kinetic Warm-Up: Play *Balance*. Ask students to stand, raise their hands above their heads, and bend over slowly and gently touch their toes. Let everyone gently stretch out their spines and then slowly stand up. Invite everyone to concentrate on tightening the core or center of their body and slowly lifting one leg from the ground. Practice balancing on each leg.

Vocal Warm-Up: Allow students to improvise neutral responses in pairs to another person's request to take sides. For example:

- I'd rather not get involved.
- I can listen but I can't really comment. I wasn't there.
- I don't know what he/she is thinking.

Conversation Starter Questions:

- Has someone ever pressured you to take sides in an argument? How did you handle it at the time?
- How do you wish you had handled it?

Role-Play Ideas: Invite three students into the playing area to role-play these scenarios.

- Friend 1 says to Friend 2 that Friend 3 didn't invite him/her to a party. Friend 3 says to Friend 2 that he/she did. Both Friend 1 and Friend 3 try to persuade Friend 2 to take their side.
- A mother complains to her child that it is the father's fault that they are divorcing. The father complains to the child that it is the mother's fault.

Freeze Ideas: In each case, freeze and ask the class how the cornered party can stay neutral.

- What can be said or done to support the people talking without getting drawn into the conflict?

Revise, Refine, Redo: Redo with each cornered party actually taking sides. Observe and discuss how this damages relationships.

Everybody Practice: Allow the class to role-play these same scenarios in groups of three and practice coming up with neutral statements.

Wrapping It Up—Synthesis Questions:

- How might the negative thinking patterns of *judgment, mind reading,* and *magnifying* get in the way of being neutral?
- How will being neutral improve your relationships?
- How could failing to remain neutral damage them?

PERSISTENCE

Competency: Self-Management

Track: Listening to Our Minds

Definition: Persistence is staying the course even when we are presented with difficulties.

Detailed Description: Most of us have hopes, dreams, and goals for ourselves. Some of these are short term (*I hope to spend some time outside today*) and some of them are long term (*I hope to buy my own house one day*). But, it is not always a simple path to fulfilling our dreams or reaching our goals. We may give up if we don't develop persistence. In order to persist when things get difficult, we need to:

- Keep our end goal in mind
- Remind ourselves why this dream or end goal is important to us
- Stay flexible about various ways that we might be able to reach this goal

Kinetic Warm-Up: Play *Point of Focus*. Invite students to sit quietly, calm their bodies, and begin deep and gentle breathing. They may count their breaths or breathe gently and observe their "busy minds." Instead of closing their eyes fully, students should close them halfway and gently focus on a specific point about four feet in front of them. This could be the pattern on a rug, a doorknob, or even rays of sunlight. Ask them to use this as a point of focus during deep breathing/meditation.

Vocal Warm-Up: Ask students to talk in pairs about a short-term goal and how they plan to accomplish it.

Conversation Starter Questions:

- How might it help us to persist if we remind ourselves why our dream or goal is important to us?
- Why might it help us to persist if we keep our end goal in mind?
- Why might it be important to stay flexible about how we reach our goals?

Role-Play Ideas: Invite two or more students to role-play a conversation about [*practicing an instrument/learning a new language/getting a part-time job/running for student government/changing what they eat*]. Make sure that one or more of the characters is persistent and the others want to give up.

Freeze Ideas: Ask the character who wants to give up if they can articulate the reasons that this dream or goal is important to them. Ask if the class notices any difference in the body language of the character(s) who wants to persist and those who want to give up.

Revise, Refine, Redo: Do a version where the character(s) who wants to give up tries to convince those who want to persist that giving up is a better choice. What reasons do they provide?

Everybody Practice: Ask students to talk in pairs and articulate why the short-term dream or goal that they shared earlier is important to them and how they might stay flexible in reaching it.

Wrapping It Up — Synthesis Questions:

- At what point might it be helpful to remember why a dream or goal is important to you?
- What does it mean to stay flexible in your plan to reach your goal?

UNDERSTANDING ANGER

Competency: Self-Management

Track: Listening to Our Emotions

Definition: Anger is an emotion characterized by antagonism or hostility toward someone or something you feel has deliberately done you wrong.

Detailed Description: Anger is a familiar emotion, but have we taken time to understand how anger affects us, and how our anger may affect other people? The cause of our anger is a sense that our basic emotional needs—safety, security, belonging, respect, and love—have been violated and that the people who violated them do not care.

Kinetic Warm-Up: Play *Dancing Anger*. Anger creates a strong physical energy within us. Invite students to move their bodies in a way that demonstrates how anger moves through them. Some students may be outwardly expressive, whereas others may be very still; anger moves through us all differently.

Vocal Warm-Up: Using a distributive talk technique, ask students to share something that often ignites their anger. For example, a student might say, "when people lie to me" or "when my parents ground me."

Conversation Starter Questions: When someone violates our basic emotional needs of safety, security, belonging, respect, and love, we often experience other emotions before we experience anger. We may feel confused or rejected. If we communicate these emotions and others listen, we likely will not get angry, but if we are ignored we often will.

- Can you think of a time when you became very angry?
- What basic emotional need was violated and what emotions did you experience before you became angry?

Role-Play Ideas: Invite one student to play a principal, another to play a student with a hat, and additional students to play peers in the hallway. The principal will ask the student to take off his/her hat in the hallway. When the student ignores the principal, the principal will grab the hat off the student's head and the student will become outwardly angry.

Freeze Ideas: Freeze the action after the student expresses anger.

- What basic needs are being violated for both principal and student?
- How might the student or principal express their other emotions before becoming angry?

Revise, Refine, Redo: Redo the role-play and have a student remind their friend about the "no hat" rule.

- Does this inspire the same amount of anger on both sides? Why or why not?

Everybody Practice: Invite students to role-play moments from their own lives in which they got very angry. Ask them to identify the basic emotional need that was threatened or violated and what other emotions they experienced before anger.

Wrapping It Up—Synthesis Questions:

- How can identifying the basic emotional needs that are violated help us to better understand our anger?
- How can identifying the emotions that we experience before anger help us to avoid becoming flooded with anger?
- If others do not acknowledge these other emotions, how can we acknowledge them for ourselves?

UNDERSTANDING FEAR AND ANXIETY

Competency: Self-Management

Track: Listening to Our Emotions

Definition: Fear and anxiety are emotions caused by the belief that we will experience something unpleasant or painful in our future.

Detailed Description: Like anger, fear and anxiety also come on when our basic emotional needs of safety, security, belonging, respect, and love are threatened or violated. In the case of fear and anxiety, we often have an overwhelming sense that we do not have any control over what will happen in the future, or even what is happening right now.

Kinetic Warm-Up: Play *Dancing Fear*. Fear and anxiety create a strong physical energy within us. Invite students to move their bodies in a way that demonstrates how fear or anxiety moves through them. Some students may be outwardly expressive, whereas others may be very still; fear and anxiety move through us all differently.

Vocal Warm-Up: Using a distributive talk technique, ask students to share something that often ignites their fear or anxiety. For example, a student might say, "when my friends ignore me" or "when I'm home alone."

Conversation Starter Questions: When our basic emotional needs of safety, security, belonging, respect, and love are threatened or violated, we often experience other emotions before we experience fear or anxiety. We may feel nervous or uneasy.

- Can you think of a time you became very fearful or anxious?
- What basic emotional need was violated and what emotions did you experience before you became fearful or anxious?

Role-Play Ideas: Invite two students to improvise a role-play about waiting for their parents to pick them up [*after school/at the movies/at the mall/at the park*], but their parents do not arrive.

Freeze Ideas: Pause the role-play when the characters begin to express worry.

- What basic emotional need is being threatened?
- At what point is nervousness or uneasiness turning into fear or anxiety?
- What can these characters do to remain calm?

Revise, Refine, Redo: Improvise the same situation but alter the scene so that one character is very fearful and anxious and the other is calm. How does this change the outcome of the scene?

Everybody Practice: Invite students to role-play moments from their own lives in which they got very fearful or anxious. Ask them to identify the basic emotional need that was violated and what other emotions they experienced before fear or anxiety.

Wrapping It Up—Synthesis Questions:

- How can identifying the basic emotional needs that are threatened or violated help us to better understand our fear and anxiety?
- How can identifying the emotions that we experience before our fear and anxiety help us to avoid becoming overwhelmed?
- If others do not acknowledge these other emotions, how can we acknowledge them ourselves?

UNDERSTANDING SADNESS

Competency: Self-Management

Track: Listening to Our Emotions

Definition: Sadness is an emotional pain often brought on by the loss of a relationship, of an opportunity, of an important object, or of a community.

Detailed Description: Sadness is a familiar emotion, but have we taken time to understand how sadness affects us, and how our sadness may affect other people? Sadness also comes on when our basic emotional needs of safety, security, belonging, respect, and love are threatened or violated. In the case of sadness, we often are overwhelmed by a sense of loss.

Kinetic Warm-Up: Play *Dancing Sadness*. Sadness creates a strong physical energy within us. Invite students to move their bodies in a way that demonstrates how sadness moves through them. Some students may be outwardly expressive, whereas others may be very still; sadness moves through us all differently.

Vocal Warm-Up: Using a distributive talk technique, ask students to share something that brings on their sadness. For example, a student might say, "when someone dies" or "when I'm not chosen for a team."

Conversation Starter Questions: When our basic emotional needs of safety, security, belonging, respect, and love are threatened or violated, we often experience other emotions before we experience sadness. We may experience denial, or the sense that this could not be true.

- Can you think of a time you became very sad?
- What basic emotional need was threatened and what emotions did you experience before you became sad?

Role-Play Ideas: Invite two students to improvise a role-play where one of them learns that their [*cat/dog/grandparent*] has died.

Freeze Ideas: Pause the role-play after the affected character receives the bad news.

- What basic emotional need is being threatened?
- At what point is denial turning into sadness?
- What can these characters do to deal with the sadness?

Revise, Refine, Redo: Improvise the same situation but alter the scene so that one character refuses to believe the news.

- What can the other character do to help them face their sadness and loss?

Everybody Practice: Invite students to role-play moments from their own lives in which they got very sad. Ask them to identify the basic emotional need that was violated and what other emotions they experienced before their sadness.

Wrapping It Up—Synthesis Questions:

- How can identifying the basic emotional needs that are threatened or violated help us to better understand our sadness?
- How can identifying the emotions that we experience before our sadness help us to cope with the sadness itself?
- If others do not acknowledge these other emotions, how can we acknowledge them?

COPING STRATEGIES FOR ANGER, FEAR, AND SADNESS

Competency: Self-Management

Track: Listening to Our Emotions

Definition: Anger, fear, and sadness are three of our six basic emotions, and they all bring with them strong experiences that can be hard to manage. Learning some specific coping strategies can be helpful when we are faced with the strong experiences of anger, fear, and sadness.

Detailed Description: Understanding that anger, fear, and sadness are all brought on by the sense that our basic emotional needs of safety, security, belonging, respect, and love are being threatened or violated is a good starting point for coping with these emotions. Understanding that we often experience other, less intense emotions before these stronger emotions come on can also help us to understand what we are feeling before being engulfed by the strong emotions of anger, fear, and sadness. But, sometimes the intensity of anger, fear, and sadness are unavoidable. Beyond understanding underlying causes of these emotions, what can we do to cope with them?

Kinetic Warm-Up: Play *Let It Go*. Invite students to stand, stretch their arms above their heads, and take a deep breath in. As they exhale invite them to slowly bend their torso over their legs. When they have completely exhaled, invite them to hang over their legs and stretch out their backs while taking two to three gentle breaths in and out. Repeat this cycle two or three times.

Vocal Warm-Up: Invite students to share in small groups or pairs some familiar coping strategies that can help them deal with the intense feelings of anger, fear, and sadness.

Conversation Starter Questions: We already know about some coping strategies for dealing with anger, fear, and sadness. Taking deep breaths, meditating to stop our "busy minds," and practicing positive self-talk can all help us to cope with the intensity of anger, fear, and sadness.

- Can you think of a time when you were overcome with intense anger, fear, or sadness?
- Were you able to calm yourself? If not, in hindsight what strategies do you think might have been helpful?

Role-Play Ideas:

- *Coping with anger:* Revisit the role-play about the principal and the student who is wearing a hat in the hallway. In this version, imagine that the character of the student uses self-talk to calm down before or after becoming angry. Ask, "What could this student say to him/herself to calm down and deal with the situation?"

- *Coping with fear*: Revisit the role-play about waiting for parents who do not arrive for a pickup. In this version, imagine that the characters practice deep breathing to calm their minds before or after becoming overwhelmed with fear. Ask, "How might it help them to calm their minds and make a good decision in this moment?"
- *Coping with sadness*: Revisit the role-play where one character learns that their [*cat/dog/grandparent*] has died. In this version, imagine that the character practices deep breathing and positive self-talk to help them accept their loss. Ask, "Why might it be helpful to practice both deep breathing and positive self-talk?"

Freeze Ideas: Call "freeze" and ask the audience to observe the bodies of the actors at various points in the role-play, both before and after the coping techniques have been used.

- Do the characters appear calmer before or after using these strategies?
- What do the bodies of the characters reveal about the effectiveness of these coping strategies?

Revise, Refine, Redo: Repeat these role-plays using different coping strategies for each scenario. For example, use deep breathing for coping with anger and self-talk for coping with fear.

Everybody Practice: Invite students to practice in pairs, with each student recalling a moment in their own life when they were angry, fearful, or sad. Ask each student to choose the technique of deep breathing, meditating to calm a "busy mind," or positive self-talk, or they may choose a combination of all three. Finally, with their partner, each student should role-play this moment from their own life using one or more of the coping strategies.

Wrapping It Up—Synthesis Questions: We can practice deep breathing, meditation to calm our "busy minds," and positive self-talk to help us calm down *before* we become angry, fearful, or sad. We can also practice these coping strategies *after* we have been overwhelmed by these feelings.

- What are the benefits and challenges of using these strategies *before* we are overwhelmed with the intensity of these feelings?
- What are the benefits and challenges of using these strategies *after* we are overwhelmed with the intensity of these feelings?

UNDERSTANDING BIAS

Competency: Self-Management

Track: Listening to Our Environment

Definition: Biases are unconscious preferences we form based on associations between various objects, ideas, and people.

Detailed Description: We all have biases that are based on associations that are presented to us repeatedly and over time through the media, education, and social interactions. For example, many of us associate salt and pepper, day and night, and peanut butter and jelly. These examples involve objects and are fairly harmless, meaning it does not hurt peanut butter or jelly if we prefer to eat them together, nor does it hurt day if we pair it with night.

But when we associate people who look like us with the idea of being trustworthy, we may favor them and give them advantages. And, if we associate people who don't look like us with certain negative qualities or ideas, we may deny them opportunities.

Kinetic Warm-Up: Play *Quick Change*. Invite students to call out any simple physical exercise for the group. Any student may call "Switch" and name another exercise whenever they like. With each exercise the group will switch and change what they are doing until the next switch is called. For example, "Run in place"—*SWITCH*—"Jumping jacks"—*SWITCH*—"Deep breathing"—*SWITCH*—"Stretch over your legs."

Vocal Warm-Up: Play *Rapid-Fire Word Association*. Invite students to work in pairs. One student will say any word that comes to their mind and their partner will say the first word that they associate with it. Have the students quickly switch roles and repeat. Continue this pattern for at least ten cycles. Students should do this quickly, without thinking, to discover together some of their habitual associations.

Conversation Starter Questions: Though biases often form the basis of stereotype or prejudice, they are different than stereotype or prejudice in that they do not necessarily reflect strongly held beliefs. Though we associate peanut butter with jelly and may prefer to eat them together, we likely don't have a strong belief or conviction that this is the best or only use of peanut butter or jelly. Our preference is more a reflection of our habitual association of the two than our convictions.

- What two people, things, or ideas do you always see associated with one another?
- Why do you believe that these two people, things, or ideas are always presented together?

On the other hand, sometimes our biases affect our behavior in a way that makes us prefer some people over others for no good reason. There was a time in history when all orchestras were filled with male musicians. Female musicians stated that they believed they were not being hired because there was a bias that associated men, rather than women, with great musicianship. Female musicians fought to have blind auditions that took place behind a screen so that the judge could not tell if a man or woman was playing, and now orchestras have many female players.

- What did the judges learn about themselves and their own biases after engaging in the blind auditions?

Role-Play Ideas: There is bias in our country that associates the word "immigrants" with the word "illegal." Invite students to improvise a role-play about a student who has moved from another country. How would his fellow students act if they associated "immigrants" with "illegal"? How would his fellow students act if they did not associate "immigrants" with "illegal"?

Freeze Ideas: Freeze the role-play at the moment the students' bias becomes clear.

- What is the new student thinking and feeling when he/she is confronted with the idea that some people associate "immigrants" and "illegal"?
- How could the new student respond when confronted with this kind of bias?

Revise, Refine, Redo: Redo the role-play and have a large group of new students who are refugees arrive at the school together.

- How does it change the dynamic between students who see immigrants as illegal if there is a large group of new students who all share the same story?

Everybody Practice: Invite students to work in small groups or pairs and discuss the problems it causes in our society when "immigrants" and "illegal" are linked in our minds.

Wrapping It Up—Synthesis Questions: We all have biases, which are just associations that are formed through repetition in the media, education, and society. But, when these associations are negative ideas that we associate with other people, they can affect how we treat one another.

- What can we all do to become aware of our biases?
- What can we do to dismantle them?

UNDERSTANDING STEREOTYPES

Competency: Self-Management

Track: Listening to Our Environment

Definition: Stereotypes are recognizable patterns of behavior that we assume are true for all members of a particular group.

Detailed Description: Stereotypes are simply patterns we recognize. They are neutral, neither positive nor negative in and of themselves. For instance, "Basketball players are tall" and "Lots of moms drive minivans" are both neutral statements that recognize patterns in a particular group. The problem with stereotypes occurs when we assume that these patterns of behavior apply to *all* individual members of a group. If we say "All tall people play basketball" or "All moms drive minivans," we are stereotyping tall people and moms by applying general ideas to all members of a group.

Words like "all" and "everyone" are tipoffs to the use of a stereotype. Whether a stereotype conveys a positive generalization or a negative generalization, the act of stereotyping others is damaging, as no one idea accurately describes all the individual members of a group.

Kinetic Warm-Up: Play *Everyone*. Invite students to stand and gently walk around the perimeter of the circle or playing area. Slowly increase the speed of the walking to a very gentle jog. Finally, increase it to a slow run. The goal is to have everyone move at the same pace and the same time. Then slow the run to a jog and the jog to a walk until everyone reaches their seats.

Vocal Warm-Up: Invite students to talk in pairs or groups about the various social groups of which they are a part: boys, girls, soccer players, band members, recent immigrants, ethnic groups, cultural groups, gamers, etc. Invite them to speak about the stereotypes that are attached to the particular groups of which they are a part and how these stereotypes affect them personally.

Conversation Starter Questions: Stereotypes, though they just recognize patterns of behavior in a group, are always problematic, as no one idea can be accurately applied to all members of a group.

- How can positive stereotypes actually have a negative effect on the members of a group?
- How does the act of stereotyping affect the person who holds the stereotype in their mind?

Role-Play Ideas: Invite students to role-play a scenario where a teacher stereotypes an Asian student by believing that all Asian students are great at math and therefore brushes off their math questions. Invite students to role-play a scenario where a Latin American student is asked to tutor his/her white friends for their Spanish test because they believe the stereotype "All Latin Americans speak Spanish," even though this particular student does not speak Spanish.

Freeze Ideas: Freeze the scene at the moment that there is obvious confusion between the person who is being stereotyped and the person who is stereotyping.

- How do stereotypes cause confusion and miscommunication between people?
- What emotions may be triggered for the person who is being stereotyped?

Revise, Refine, Redo: Redo each role-play and remove the stereotyping from the exchanges, meaning the teacher does not assume that the Asian student is great at math and the white students do not assume that the Latin American student speaks Spanish.

- How does the relationship between the teacher and the Asian student change when the teacher *does not* assume he/she is great at math?
- How does the student's ability to learn in the classroom improve?
- How does the relationship between the white students and the Latin American student change when the white students *do not* assume he/she speaks Spanish?

Everybody Practice: Refer to the earlier conversation that students had in the vocal warm-up about a time that they had been stereotyped by others based on being a member of a certain group. Invite students to think about what they could say to someone who is stereotyping them. A simple formula for responding to stereotyping is to acknowledge your membership in a group and then counter the stereotype by letting the speaker know that not all members of that group share the characteristic expressed in the stereotype. For example, a student might say, "I am Latin American, but not all Latin Americans speak Spanish."

Wrapping It Up—Synthesis Questions: Stereotypes are simply generalizations applied to all members of a group. They may be based on biases. They may be positive or they may be negative, but they always cause miscommunication because all members of a group cannot be accurately described by one characteristic.

- Who have you stereotyped?

- How might you change your own thinking so that you do not stereotype others?

PERSONAL SPACE

Competency: Social Awareness

Track: Listening to Our Bodies

Definition: Personal space is the amount of space around our body that we need to feel comfortable.

Detailed Description: There is no standard amount of space that a person needs around their own body in order to feel comfortable. Everyone is different and what feels comfortable for one person may not feel comfortable for another. Some people are close talkers, whereas others keep their distance, and some people's standard greeting is a hug, others a handshake or a nod and a smile. Since we all have different personal space needs and preferences, it is important to take some time to understand and learn to communicate our own personal space needs and to learn to sense and respond to the personal space needs of others.

Kinetic Warm-Up: Play *Mirror Games*. Invite students to work in pairs. They should sit in chairs facing one another. One person is designated the leader and will make a series of movements or gestures. The follower will mimic the leader's movements or gestures and try to stay in perfect sync with them. The leader should take care not to move too fast, or they will be impossible to follow. Switch roles after one to two minutes and allow the follower to lead and the leader to follow.

Vocal Warm-Up: Invite students to talk in groups about the amount of personal space that they personally need in order to feel comfortable. Encourage them to be specific, by using measurements in inches or feet and showing people with their hands. Encourage them to acknowledge the different preferences within their group without judgment.

Conversation Starter Questions: Invite students to share their different personal space preferences within the larger group.

- Why do you prefer _____ amount of personal space?
- Are your own preferences for personal space similar to or different than people in your family? How?

Role-Play Ideas: Invite two students to role-play a conversation between a "close talker" character, or someone who likes to lean in and look directly in someone's eyes when they are sharing, and a "keep your distance" character who likes to maintain at least three feet of space between themselves and others and does not make eye contact.

Freeze Ideas: Ask students to observe and describe the body language of both characters. Ask students to observe and describe the differences in eye contact for each character.

- What do the body language and eye contact tell you about how this character is feeling?

Revise, Refine, Redo: Redo this role-play with two "close talker" characters and with two "keep your distance" characters.

- How does the dynamic of the conversation change?

Everybody Practice: Ask students to return to the group they were in during the vocal warm-up, where they shared their personal space needs. Ask them to improvise conversations between people in their own group who have different personal space preferences.

- What do we need to do to become more aware of others' personal space needs?
- How can we adjust our communication so that everyone feels comfortable?

Wrapping It Up—Synthesis Questions: We all have different personal space preferences. If we are not aware of our own personal space preferences and the preferences of others, we might have unnecessary misunderstandings or conflict.

- How can we better communicate our own personal space preferences to others?
- What cues in body language and eye contact will help us to recognize the personal space needs of others even if they are not directly communicated?
- How can we remain flexible so that we are comfortable and those around us are comfortable when communicating?

NONVERBAL COMMUNICATION

Competency: Social Awareness

Track: Listening to Our Bodies

Definition: Nonverbal communication is all the information we send and receive through wordless cues.

Detailed Description: Nonverbal communication includes nuances of body language and tone of voice such as eye contact and eye movement, physical gestures, distance between people, speed with which someone speaks, softness or loudness of the voice, and emotionality of the voice. Psychologists talk about the importance of nonverbal communication, and Professor Albert Mehrabian famously theorized that our nonverbal communication has as much or *more* weight in communicating our message than our words.

Nonverbal communication can give us clues to the true meaning and intent of someone's words, especially in cases where the meaning and intent of the words do not match the body language and tone of voice. Learning to read nonverbal cues, and being aware of the nonverbal cues that we are sending, particularly if our verbal and nonverbal communication is incongruous, can improve our relationships with others.

Kinetic Warm-Up: Play *Opposites*. Ask students to stand. The group will participate in an altered version of charades where students make a physical tableau that is the opposite of the emotional label it is given. For instance, you or a student calls out the word "frustrated" and individuals in the class make physical tableaus that communicate "satisfied." Other examples of opposites include fearful/confident, worried/secure, annoyed/pleased, hateful/loving, and confused/clear.

Vocal Warm-Up: Have students work in small groups to play a version of *Opposites* that focuses on vocal tone. In this version, students will say a nonemotional sentence such as "Please pass the potatoes" or "Can you turn on the lights?" or "It's getting late" with as many emotional vocal tones as possible. Can these sentences be said with anger, frustration, joyfulness, fear, annoyance, worry, or love?

Conversation Starter Questions: The power of our nonverbal communication is often what makes us believe or disbelieve someone's message. Some people sound annoyed all the time; even if they say that they are excited, it is hard to believe them. Others are so enthusiastic that we miss the hints they give about being upset.

- Have you ever doubted what someone says based on the way they say it?

- Have you ever contradicted your own words with body language or a vocal tone that does not match your meaning?

Role-Play Ideas: Invite two students to role-play a scenario where one character asks another character if they want to hang out and do a certain activity [*student choice*]. The second character says, "Yeah, sure. Sounds great," but says these, or other similar improvised sentences, with a body language and vocal tone that convey the opposite. Invite students to improvise a scenario between two people who do not speak the same language and one of them needs directions to the post office.

Freeze Ideas: Freeze the first role-play at a point when the second character's body language clearly displays feelings that contradict the affirmative message they are sending.

- What feeling does this character's body language convey?
- What would their body language look like if it matched their verbal communication?
- How did the second character's vocal tone contradict the meaning of their words?

In the case of the second suggested role-play:

- How can nonverbal communication be as effective as verbal communication?

Revise, Refine, Redo: Redo the first role-play so that the nonverbal and verbal communication are congruous, or matching.

- How does this reinforcement of the same message verbally and nonverbally affect the communication between the two people and their relationship?

Everybody Practice: Invite students to work in pairs on a version of the role-play where one character invites another to hang out. Ask them to run the role-play matching the verbal and nonverbal communication and reflect upon how that affects the relationship between their characters. Then ask them to play with incongruities between the verbal and nonverbal communication. Ask them to reflect on how incongruities between verbal and nonverbal communication affect the relationship overall.

Wrapping It Up—Synthesis Questions: If we want to understand others, we need to learn to read their verbal as well as their nonverbal communication. Sometimes nonverbal communication is even more powerful than verbal communication when it comes to clarifying a message. If we want to be fully understood by others, it is helpful if our verbal and nonverbal communication match.

- What can you do to make your verbal and nonverbal communication align with one another more closely?
- How will doing so positively affect your relationships?

CODE-SWITCHING

Competency: Social Awareness

Track: Listening to Our Minds

Definition: "Code-switching" refers to the way we adjust our verbal and nonverbal communication styles to better fit into any given cultural context or group.

Detailed Description: "Code-switching" is a term that originated in the field of linguistics and originally referred to the way in which multilingual people switch between languages or use words from multiple languages in creative ways. The term is now popularly used to express the way we all switch our verbal and nonverbal communication to match the cultural context or group of which we are a part.

We all code-switch on a daily basis. For instance, we all speak in one way to a shop owner and another way with our friends. We might code-switch with our choice of words, tone of voice, body language, or manner of dressing. We code-switch for different reasons: to share a laugh with someone, to better connect with someone, to show respect to someone, to build trust with someone, to protect ourselves, to hide parts of our identity, or to reveal parts of our identity.

While we all code-switch, some of us are required to code-switch more often than others. For instance, it is well known that many professional environments expect people to "talk white," or in a manner that reflects white or European American culture. This may require people of color to adapt or hide their own cultural dialect in order to fit in or even to get a job.

Kinetic Warm-Up: Play *Dance Party*. Using a digital music source, play thirty- to forty-five-second segments from musical pieces that represent diverse musical cultures. Invite students to dance to any and all music that resonates with them. Be sure to represent many different cultures in your choices: hip-hop, Latin, country, rock, blues, gospel, reggaeton, punk, etc.

Vocal Warm-Up: Invite students to work in small groups. Ask them to brainstorm and come up with as many different ways of greeting someone as they can. Then ask them to discuss why they would choose one greeting over another.

Conversation Starter Questions: In the United States, we live in a diverse country where people speak in various regional dialects. People from the South speak differently from people in the Northeast and the West. Within those regions are other accents that are specific to states, towns, or even neighborhoods. Furthermore, we are a nation of immigrants, and our manner of speaking is informed not just by where we live but by the cultures from which we came.

At the same time, there are messages that we receive through media and education about the "right way to talk" or the "right way to act," and sometimes our most natural way of speaking or carrying ourselves may be seen by others as incorrect.

- Have you ever felt like your way of talking or carrying yourself is "not correct"?
- Who gave you the message that you should change your way of speaking or acting to fit in better?
- Have you ever changed your way of speaking or acting in order to fit in?

Role-Play Ideas: Invite students to role-play a scene where one character is attending a job interview. Invite one student to play the character of the interviewer, who speaks and acts in a "professional manner," and the other to play the interviewee, who speaks and acts in a manner that does not match the tone set by the interviewer. Invite students to improvise another role-play among an ethnically mixed group of friends who all greet each other multiple times in order to reflect and respect all of their cultural backgrounds.

Freeze Ideas: Freeze the first role-play and ask students to describe the differences in the body language of both characters. Ask students to describe the differences in the verbal communication and the vocal tone of each character. For the second role-play, ask students to talk about the pleasure of code-switching among friends.

Revise, Refine, Redo: Redo the first scene and have the interviewee switch their code so that they speak in a way that matches the environment or mirrors the style of the interviewer.

- How does the interview go when the interviewee matches the style of the interviewer?
- Does the interviewee get better results or worse results when they match the communication style of the interviewer?

Everybody Practice: Invite students to work in pairs. Parents and children often speak in different languages and parents do not often understand the slang that their children use. Have one student play the character of a parent and the other student play their child, and invite them to improvise a conversation where the parent misunderstands the child's slang. Then have the parent code-switch and actually use the child's slang correctly.

Wrapping It Up—Synthesis Questions: We all code-switch throughout our day, most of the time to connect with the people around us. But, there are times when we need to code-switch in order to protect ourselves or expand our opportunities.

- What is a situation in which you might need to code-switch in order to protect yourself?
- How can we get better at code-switching in our own lives?

COGNITIVE EMPATHY

Competency: Social Awareness

Track: Listening to Our Minds

Definition: Empathy is the ability to understand and share the feelings of another.

Detailed Description: Empathy is often presented as a personal quality that some of us have and others don't. But we can also look at empathy as a set of related skills that we can all develop. Social scientists suggest that there are three different types of empathy: cognitive, emotional, and compassionate.

Cognitive empathy is the ability to understand someone else's situation and point of view, and it can be developed through various storytelling games, through literature, through travel, through conversation, or through discussions around current events or history. Developing our cognitive empathy involves engaging our imagination so that we can envision the circumstances and challenges of someone else's life in detail. In common terms, we call it "putting ourselves in someone else's shoes."

Kinetic Warm-Up: Play *Walk in My Shoes.* Everyone has a different way of walking. Some of us walk quickly, others more slowly. Some of us have long strides, others short strides. Have students work in pairs. Invite one partner to walk around the room. The other partner will observe their gait. They will then attempt to walk behind their partner, exactly mimicking their gait. Allow students to switch so that the observer becomes the observed and each partner gets a chance to "walk in the other's shoes."

Vocal Warm-Up: Give students thirty to sixty seconds to recall a time when they felt scared, then ask them to find a partner. Ask each pair to decide on the first speaker and let them know they will have one to two minutes to share their story. When they are finished, ask the listeners to paraphrase the situation, identify the details that made this situation so scary, and identify the moment in the story when the speaker felt most afraid. Switch and let the speaker become the listener.

Conversation Starter Questions: The key to developing our cognitive empathy is our imagination. If we can imagine someone else's life in detail, we can express that we understand the struggles they may be experiencing.

- Name a character from literature who has a different life than you. How is their life different than yours?
- How is it the same as yours?

Role-Play Ideas: Invite two students into the playing area to interview one another about a time they were very angry. The first speaker will have one to two minutes to share their story. When they are finished, the listener will paraphrase the situation, identify the details that made their partner so angry, and identify the moment in the story when the speaker felt the angriest.

Ask the speakers to reflect on their partner's retelling of their story and consider these questions:

- Did the listener describe the situation accurately? If not, can you clarify their understanding?
- Did the listener understand the details that made you so angry? If not, can you clarify their understanding?
- Did the listener understand the moment that made you the angriest? If not, can you clarify their understanding?

Freeze Ideas: Freeze the role-play when a listener has obviously missed an important detail of the speaker's story. Ask the class to help them recall that detail. Freeze the role-play if a listener does not correctly identify the moment in the story that most affected the speaker. Ask the class to help clarify their understanding.

Revise, Refine, Redo: Switch and let the speaker become the listener. Repeat the role-play with two new students.

Everybody Practice: Have students work in pairs or groups to complete this sentence: "The one thing no one ever understands about me or my life is _____." Invite other group members to practice cognitive empathy by getting more information about this situation, accurately paraphrasing the information they receive, and clearly identifying key details of the situation.

Wrapping It Up—Synthesis Questions: Cognitive empathy boils down to understanding someone else's point to view. To do this, listen closely to their story and envision details as they speak, then identify and paraphrase the key details. Make sure that you are clear about why the speaker feels the way they do.

- Is there someone in your life who might feel misunderstood?
- Could you ask them to tell you their story and practice cognitive empathy with them?

RULES AND NORMS

Competency: Social Awareness

Track: Listening to Our Emotions

Definition: Rules are a set of clearly understood and communicated expectations for behavior that usually have explicit consequences if ignored or broken. Norms are patterns of behavior that are typical of a particular group, change over time, and do not have explicit consequences if ignored or broken.

Detailed Description: Rules and norms are not the same thing, but it is important to be aware of them both. Rules are often decided by people in authority, written out so that everyone understands them, and have some form of explicit consequences if they are ignored or broken. These consequences may be a punishment of some sort, like detention, or a request to repair a situation with some offering, like an apology.

Norms are unwritten, and often not even openly discussed, agreements on how a group of people behaves. Norms can evolve and change over time. One way that people keep power over others is by refusing to clearly communicate norms and setting up an "insider/outsider" culture based on who knows the norms and who does not.

Kinetic Warm-Up: Play *Simon Says*, a simple game that humorously looks at the social norm of following rules and what happens when we are unable to. Invite different students to lead.

Vocal Warm-Up: Invite students to talk in small groups or pairs about rules that they understand and those that they don't, or rules that they wish they could change.

Conversation Starter Questions:

- If rules are clearly communicated and often decided by people in authority, can we brainstorm some rules we all follow? (e.g., *We all stay in class until the period is over. We do not steal other people's property.*)
- If norms are unspoken agreements among members of a certain group and are often changing, can we brainstorm some norms that we are aware of and follow? (e.g., *We usually dress according to our gender. We usually say "please" and "thank you" when borrowing someone else's things.*)

Role-Play Ideas: Invite students to improvise a role-play on what happens if someone breaks the social norm of waiting in line [*in the lunchroom/grocery store/movie theater*]. Invite students to improvise another role-play on what happens if someone breaks the social norm of dressing according to their gender or wearing clothes appropriate for the environment (e.g., pajamas to school, ball gown to a baseball game).

Freeze Ideas: Freeze the action when other characters notice the character who is ignoring or breaking with social norms.

- What do the faces and body language of the other people say about their willingness to accept someone who breaks social norms?

Revise, Refine, Redo: Redo the role-plays and flip the norm and the breaking of the norm. For example, assume that no one waits in line and it breaks the social norm to ask others to form a line, or that no one wears gendered clothes and it breaks the social norm to dress according to your gender.

- What does this experiment tell us about social norms?

Everybody Practice: Invite students to talk in groups or pairs about good reasons we might have to break social norms. Have them devise role-plays where they break a social norm for a good reason and have them explain this reason to the other characters in the role-play. For example, a character might say, "I'm sorry to ask if I can cut the lunch line, but I need to meet with my teacher during lunch and he/she asked me to hurry," or "I don't dress according to any gender because I believe people can wear whatever they want."

Wrapping It Up—Synthesis Questions:

- Why might it be important to pay attention to the rules and norms in a new environment?
- If we want to ignore or break certain norms, for what responses should we prepare ourselves?
- If we feel we have a good reason to break with a social norm, what inner qualities might we need in order to succeed without being hurt by the rejection or judgment of others?

EMOTIONAL DISPLAY RULES

Competency: Social Awareness

Track: Listening to Our Emotions

Definition: Emotional display rules are the social norms and etiquette for how, when, and where to express or not express emotions. Emotional display styles are the ways we choose to express our emotions, either animatedly or more calmly.

Detailed Description: Our social groups and norms influence everything from our choice of clothing and our choice of words to the way we choose to display our emotions. For some cultures, a funeral is a celebration full of laughter and music, whereas for others it is a somber affair where laughter would be considered inappropriate. In some cultures, people kiss each other on the cheek to say goodbye, but in others they wave. In some cultures, using lots of gestures and speaking loudly is interpreted as passion and commitment, whereas in others it is interpreted as disrespectful. In many cultures, boys are told they should never cry, but in others there is less restriction on boys and crying. In many cultures, girls are not supposed to display anger, but in others there is less restriction on girls and anger.

All of these rules are unwritten norms and they can produce misunderstandings between people. They can also make anyone feel pressure when the way they feel inside does not match the emotional display rules of their environment.

Kinetic Warm-Up: Play *Not What It Looks Like*. Students stand in a circle. One student starts by pantomiming an action while stating that they are doing something different than what the action conveys. For instance, the student may pantomime the action of sewing with a needle and thread while saying, "I'm running to work." The following person pantomimes the action that was described by the previous person, while stating that they are doing something different than what the action conveys. For example, the following person would pantomime the action of running to work while saying, "I'm eating pizza."

Vocal Warm-Up: Have students work in pairs or small groups and share a time when they were given a message that they should not express the emotions that they were genuinely feeling.

Conversation Starter Questions: We all experience our emotions differently. Not everyone expresses anger, sadness, fear, or joy in the same way. Some of us tend to be more animated when we express our emotions and some of us tend to be calmer. To add to the confusion, we get messages from our environment, social groups, and cultures about acceptable way to express our emotions, and sometimes our tendencies for emotional expression may not align with these messages.

- What are the emotional display rules in your family?
- Do you feel like the emotional display rules in your family fit well with your personality, or do you find yourself expressing emotion in a way that leads to misunderstandings?
- Are the emotional display rules in your family similar to other environments you find yourself in, or do you need to adjust how you express your emotions outside of your home?

Role-Play Ideas: Invite a group of students in the playing area to improvise a conversation at a dinner table in a family that has a very animated emotional display style.

Freeze Ideas: Freeze the role-play and ask the class to describe the way this family expresses their emotions.

- What gestures and tone of voice did the characters in this improv use to show that they had an animated emotional display style?

Revise, Refine, Redo: Suggest that one character in the family dinner improvisation adopt a calm emotional display style, rather than an animated emotional display style. Redo the role-play.

- What happens between the characters when one of them has a different emotional display style?
- Do conflicts or misunderstandings occur?

Everybody Practice: Ask students to work in pairs and have a conversation where they play two characters with two different emotional display styles—one animated and one more calm. How does their conversation flow? How do they navigate the misunderstandings that come from having different emotional display styles?

Wrapping It Up—Synthesis Questions: We all have certain emotional display styles that we have learned and that suit our personalities. Some of these come from our families and cultures. When our emotional display style contrasts with the emotional display rules in our environment, we can have misunderstandings.

- Have you ever gotten in trouble in school for expressing emotions in a way that other people felt was inappropriate?
- What do you wish other people understood about the way you express your emotions that they do not understand now?
- How might you change the way you express your emotions in different environments so that you will have fewer misunderstandings?

UNDERSTANDING PREJUDICE

Competency: Social Awareness

Track: Listening to Our Environment

Definition: Prejudices are thoughts, feelings, and attitudes that are negative in tone or content that we hold about an individual or group with which we are unfamiliar. Prejudice is literally the act of prejudging an individual or a group without having experience with, or reliable information about, them.

Detailed Description: Prejudices are often built upon bias and stereotype, but they are always solidified by a lack of actual experience with or information about a particular group or its members. Prejudices are always negative thoughts, feelings, or attitudes that convey a deep dislike of a person or people based on uninformed assumptions about the group to which they belong. In our country, which is made of Native Americans, Hawaiian and Alaskan Natives, African Americans, and immigrants from almost every other country in the world, we struggle with prejudice. We should contemplate how reliable information about and experience with specific people or groups may help us reduce or eliminate our prejudices.

Kinetic Warm-Up: Play *5-4-3-2-1*. Have students organize themselves in groups of five and do five repetitions of a physical exercise of their choice. Then have them reorganize themselves in groups of four and do four repetitions of an exercise of their choice. Repeat the groupings, reducing the members in number, until everyone stands alone as one.

Vocal Warm-Up: Have students work in small groups and identify the social groups (age groups, interest groups, professional groups, religious groups, ethnic groups) they have not had much experience with and do not know much about. Allow students in the group to expand one another's experience and knowledge by sharing positive experiences and reliable information about groups with which their peers are unfamiliar.

Conversation Starter Questions: Prejudice is the act of prejudging people or groups we do not have much experience with or knowledge about.

- What groups are you a member of?
- What prejudices do other people hold about members of the groups of which you are a part?
- What would you want to say to someone who was prejudiced against you because of your membership in a particular group?

Role-Play Ideas: Invite a group of students into the playing area to improvise a scenario where a group of retired, older adults is sitting on a park bench talking about "teenagers these days."

Freeze Ideas: After the older adults expose their prejudices, freeze the role-play.

- What prejudicial attitudes do the older adults have about teenagers?
- How has their lack of experience with and knowledge of "teenagers these days" led them to misinterpret the actions of teenagers in negative way?

Revise, Refine, Redo: Invite one or two students to enter the role-play as teenagers whose behavior disproves or contradicts the prejudices that the older adults hold about "teenagers these days." Reverse the role-play and a have a group of teenagers talking about "older people." Then have one or two "older people" enter the role-play and disprove or contradict the prejudices that the teenagers hold about them.

Everybody Practice: Have students work in small groups and talk about what groups (age groups, interest groups, professional groups, religious groups, ethnic groups) they would like to learn more about. Encourage them to come up with a plan for how they can gain more experience with, and reliable information about, groups with which they are unfamiliar.

Wrapping It Up—Synthesis Questions: If we all work to step out of our comfort zones and gain more experience with individuals and groups with which we are unfamiliar, we can do our small part in fighting prejudice within our own lives.

- Who do you know and love who has prejudices against individuals and groups with which they are unfamiliar?
- How could you help someone you know and love to overcome their own prejudices?

UNDERSTANDING DISCRIMINATION

Competency: Social Awareness

Track: Listening to Our Environment

Definition: Discrimination is the specific and damaging actions taken against an individual or group based on bias, stereotypes, or prejudice.

Detailed Description: Bias, stereotypes, and prejudice are all damaging in their own ways. Bias can lead us to make unconscious associations between unrelated people and ideas, stereotypes can lead us to assume that noticeable patterns of behavior apply to all members of a given group, and prejudice can cause us to negatively judge individuals and groups with whom we are not familiar, often based on our learned biases and stereotypes. Discrimination differs from all three in that it involves specific and damaging action taken against an individual or group based on bias, stereotypes, or prejudice. This action may be verbal, emotional, physical, social, economic, or institutional. Because we live in a country where we struggle with prejudice, we also struggle with and have many examples of discrimination.

Kinetic Warm-Up: Play *Lift Me Up*. Invite students to work in groups and make tableaus of situations that represent discrimination or people organizing against discrimination. These may be drawn from their knowledge of history or from personal situations they have witnessed or experienced.

Vocal Warm-Up: There have been many situations in the history of the Unites States where people have joined together to fight against discrimination. This happens through marches, through speeches, through songs, through labor organizing, and through efforts to change laws. Invite students to talk in groups about the kinds of things that people say and do when they are organizing against discrimination.

Conversation Starter Questions:

- While bias, stereotypes, and prejudice are all damaging, discrimination may cause the most damage. Why?
- Why do you think people act in discriminatory ways against others?
- What might we be able to do to fight discrimination in our communities?

Role-Play Ideas: Return to the improvisation where some older adults sit on a park bench and express their prejudices against "teenagers these days." Explore that one of the prejudices these older adults have is that all teenagers are "up to no good." Extend the role-play by having students portray a group of teenagers who walk by the older adults. When they do, all the older adults clutch their bags close to them and say something like, "Shouldn't you be in school? What kind of trouble are you getting into? Maybe we need to call the police!"

Freeze Ideas: Freeze the role-play at the point when the older adults are saying and doing discriminatory things to the teenagers.

- What are they saying or doing that is an example of discrimination?
- Look at the faces and bodies of the teenagers. How do you think they feel when they are personally faced with discrimination based on prejudices the older adults have about teenagers in general?

Revise, Refine, Redo: Allow the role-play to continue and explore what the teenagers might say to the older adults who are discriminating against them. Revise the role-play and invite students to reenact moments in American history that demonstrate discrimination and the fight against discrimination. For example, have them re-create the sit-ins at lunch counters during the civil rights movement; the marches for farmer rights lead by Cesar Chavez; the court appearance of the Lovings, who fought for the right to marry though they were not of the same ethnicity; the creation of the AIDS quilt in Washington, DC; and/or the speeches given by Parkland students to combat gun violence in schools. In each case, have students talk and think about how the victims of discrimination feel and why the discriminators might be acting unfairly against others.

Everybody Practice: Have students work in groups and talk about times when they felt someone discriminated against them or against someone they knew. How did they respond to this incident at the time? Do they still think about this incident? If so, what do they think and feel about themselves and the world they live in as a result of this incident? Now that they understand a bit more about discrimination, how might they respond differently in the future?

Wrapping It Up—Synthesis Question: Discrimination is one of the biggest social problems that we face in the United States. We have tried for many years to remove it from our lives, but the problem persists.

- What can we all do to help end discrimination in our country?

THE POWER OF "NO"

Competency: Relationship Skills

Track: Listening to Our Bodies

Definition: Personal boundaries are guidelines or limits that a person creates for themselves so that they can clearly communicate the types of activities and interactions with which they are comfortable.

Detailed Description: We all deal with social pressures. The people around us and our larger social environment are always giving us messages about what we should do, whether these messages come from the media, our families, our peers, or people in authority. But, we are all ultimately responsible for ourselves and our own choices, no matter what pressures we face. So we need to develop strong personal boundaries so that we always act in accordance with our own deepest values.

If we have weak personal boundaries, we may say no when we mean yes or vice versa, feel guilty when we say no, do something we don't want to do in order to please others, stay silent even when we have something important to share, adopt someone else's beliefs so that we are accepted, accept physical touch that we do not want, become overly involved in someone else's problems, or allow people to speak in ways that make us uncomfortable.

Kinetic Warm-Up: Play *No-Yes*. Invite students to create their own physical gesture for "no" and their own physical gesture for "yes." Invite students to walk in the space freely, perhaps to music. When you call "freeze," or when the music stops, they should find a group of five and all make their "no" gesture in unison. Restart the music, invite students to walk freely, and when you call "freeze," or when the music stops, they should find a group of five and make their "yes" gesture in unison. Reduce the members in a group while alternating the repetition of "no" and "yes" gestures until students stand alone and perform both of their gestures on their own.

Vocal Warm-Up: Ask students to work in groups and talk about a time when they did something they did not want to do because they felt pressured by others.

Conversation Starter Questions: Most of us struggle with creating strong boundaries at some point or another in our lives. Some of us may feel we experience weak personal boundaries quite regularly and others of us might experience these things very rarely. When we do have weak personal boundaries, we might notice that we have a hard time meeting our goals because other people's priorities often pull us off track.

- What other struggles might we have if we allow ourselves to have weak personal boundaries?
- Why else might it be important to have strong personal boundaries?

Role-Play Ideas: Invite students to role-play a scene where a group of peers is trying to convince one reluctant friend to [*skip school/borrow a parent's car/take money from their parents/steal answers for a test/play a prank on a new student*].

Freeze Ideas: Freeze the scene when the group is most strongly pressuring the individual who does not want to participate.

- What does the body language of the group convey?
- What does the body language of the individual portray?
- What do you think the individual who is being pressured feels?
- What inner quality or character trait does the individual need to draw on in order to strengthen their personal boundaries?
- Why is it so hard to say no sometimes?

Revise, Refine, Redo: When other people are pressuring us, sometimes the clearest thing to do is deliver a simple "no" message. We can deliver a "nice no," which is more friendly and polite, or a "firm no," which is more serious. We may need to repeat this message more than once, and we may need to end the conversation if the message is not received. Redo the role-play and have the individual deliver a clear and simple "no" message and then walk away.

- Does this kind of simple and clear message work to change the situation?

Everybody Practice: Have students work in pairs and role-play situations where they would want to tell someone no but might feel afraid to do so. Encourage them to practice delivering a simple and clear message that strengthens their boundaries. It could be a "nice no" or a "firm no." Encourage them to repeat the message more than once, and to practice ending the conversation if the message is not received.

Wrapping It Up—Synthesis Questions:

- In what situations and with which people do you let your personal boundaries weaken?
- What fears do you have about strengthening your personal boundaries in these situations and with these people?
- How can you face those fears and make efforts to strengthen your boundaries by sending clear and simple messages?

SETTING PERSONAL BOUNDARIES

Competency: Relationship Skills

Track: Listening to Our Bodies

Definition: Personal boundaries are guidelines or limits that a person creates for themselves so that they can clearly communicate the types of activities and interactions with which they are comfortable.

Detailed Description: Learning to say no, with either a "nice no" or a "firm no," is one of the simplest ways to strengthen our personal boundaries. But, some situations are more complicated and a simple no may not be a substantial enough message to set a boundary. Sometimes people that we are close to want us to do things that we do not agree with or are not interested in. In these cases, it can be helpful to let people know that we are simply not comfortable with their idea and for that reason are not interested in participating.

If we don't strengthen our personal boundaries, even with people to whom we are close, we may feel guilty when we say no, do something we don't want to do in order to please others, stay silent even when we have something important to share, adopt someone else's beliefs so that we are accepted, accept physical touch that we do not want, become overly involved in someone else's problems, or allow people to speak in ways that make us uncomfortable.

Kinetic Warm-Up: Play *Get Comfortable*. Everyone has different comfort levels in their own bodies. Some people always wake up with a stiff neck, for example, while others wake up pain free and ready to go. Invite students to stand and stretch their bodies in whatever way makes them most comfortable.

Vocal Warm-Up: When people who are close to ask us to do things we don't want to do, we may have a hard time giving them a simple message of "no." We may feel that we want to give them more of an explanation. They may want more of an explanation, as well, and may have a hard time accepting a simple no. We need to practice saying, "I'm not comfortable with (or interested in) that," and then explaining why we are not comfortable with, or interested in, the proposed idea. In small groups, ask students to discuss other phrases that they could use to convey that they are not comfortable with or interested in doing something.

Conversation Starter Questions: When people ask us to do things that we believe are wrong, we may have trouble finding the courage and confidence to simply say no. But once we find that confidence, it is fairly easy to deliver the message. But what do we do when people ask us to do things that may not be wrong, but are not things we are not comfortable with or interested in doing?

While it may seem like it would be easier to set a clear boundary in this situation, it may be harder. Sometimes we do not want to disappoint or let down people we are close to, so we end up doing things we would rather not do in order to please them.

- Have you have been in a situation where someone you were close to asked you to do something that you were not comfortable with or interested in, and you agreed to even though you didn't want to?

Role-Play Ideas: Invite students to role-play a situation between two friends where one friend wants the other to join them in [*eating with a new group at lunch/trying out for a new club at school/talking to a teacher about finding more culturally relevant books/talking to the principal about the way a dean talks to the students/walking home on a different route/spreading the word to others about a new song or video/attending a rally against gun violence in schools*].

Freeze Ideas: Freeze the role-play at the moment when there is the most pressure or tension between the characters.

- What do you think the two characters are feeling at the moment?
- What can make it challenging to lay down a clear boundary with someone you are close to?

Revise, Refine, Redo: Expand the role-play to the point that the character who is being asked to do something that they not comfortable with lays down a clear boundary and explains their reasons for the boundary.

- When we lay down a boundary and explain our reasons for it with people to whom we are close, how does this change the conversation or the relationship?

Redo the role-play and explore what happens when the character who is pressured to do something is not able to lay down a boundary with people to whom they are close.

- How does this affect the character's feelings about themselves?
- How does this affect the relationship?

Everybody Practice: Have students work in pairs and role-play a situation between close friends where one character is pressuring another to do something they do not want to do. Encourage students to practice expressing that they are not comfortable or interested and explaining why.

Wrapping It Up—Synthesis Question: Having strong personal boundaries is just as important with people we know well as it is with people we do not know at all.

- How do you plan to strengthen your personal boundaries with people you are close to right now?

THINKING TIME

Competency: Relationship Skills

Track: Listening to Our Minds

Definition: Thinking time is the time that we need between when we are asked a question and when we are ready to respond.

Detailed Description: In classroom discussions we often hear teachers ask if students need more "thinking time," which usually means more time to come up with an answer to an academic problem or question. Most of us accept that we all require different amounts of thinking time for different academic tasks. But, we may also need different amounts of thinking time in our personal interactions.

For instance, if someone asks us to do something and we simply are not sure if we want to, we may want to ask for thinking time so that we can consider it more fully and weigh our options. Or, if someone asks us a personal question that we do not know how to answer, we may want to ask for thinking time to come up with an appropriate response. While we are used to the concept of thinking time in academic situations, the flow of social dialogue does not always allow for it. Learning to ask for thinking time in our personal interactions can help us have clear communication and strong personal boundaries.

Kinetic Warm-Up: Play *Tempo Changes*. Invite students to walk freely in the playing area. Invite students to speed up and slow down their walk at random intervals, sometimes moving at a fast walk, sometimes at a slow walk, sometimes at a light jog, and sometimes in slow motion.

Vocal Warm-Up: In the normal pace of social conversation, we are often so focused on responding to one another that we rarely consider that we are allowed to ask for thinking time. One way to do this is to simply say, "I'm not sure what I think. Can you give me a minute?" Ask students to talk in groups about other ways that they could ask for thinking time in social conversation.

Conversation Starter Questions:

- Do you ever feel pressured in social conversations to make a quick decision about [*where to go hang out/what music to listen to/where to study/whether you agree or disagree with someone*]?
- How do you usually respond when you feel pressured to make a quick decision? Do you usually go along with the majority or do you take time to make your own decision?

Role-Play Ideas: Invite students to role-play a scenario where one character is being asked to make a quick decision about [*where to go hang out/ what music to listen to/where to study/whether they agree or disagree with someone*]. Have this character practice asking for thinking time.

Freeze Ideas: Freeze the scenario after the character has asked for thinking time.

- What does the body language of the characters who were pressuring their peer to make a quick decision tell us about their feelings?
- What does the body language of the character who asked for thinking time tell us about how they feel?
- How does asking for thinking time in social conversations change the flow of dialogue between people?

Revise, Refine, Redo: Redo this role-play and run the scene with resistance to the request for thinking time.

- What can we do if people don't want to give us thinking time in social situations?
- What possible consequences do we need to prepare ourselves for if we decide to ask for thinking time?

Everybody Practice: Invite students to work in pairs and role-play a scenario where one character is pressuring another to make a quick decision about [*where to go hang out/what music to listen to/where to study/whether they agree or disagree with someone*]. Encourage students to ask for thinking time and to examine what happens in the relationship between the two characters when such a request is made.

Wrapping It Up—Synthesis Questions: Sometimes we end up doing things we don't want to do simply because we did not have time to think about our options when they were presented. Social conversations often move quickly, and there may be pressure to make a decision before we are ready.

- In what situations in your own lives might you want to ask for thinking time?
- How do you think the people in your life will respond to this request?

DO-OVERS

Competency: Relationship Skills

Track: Listening to Our Minds

Definition: A do-over is a second opportunity to do something after a previous attempt has been unsuccessful or unsatisfactory.

Detailed Description: We all have moments in our lives that do not go the way we would like them to. We may lose our temper, say something we don't mean, fail to set a clear boundary with someone, or forget a promise that we made. If we recognize that we made a mistake and would like to correct it, we can ask for a do-over.

In a do-over, we let the person know that we don't like the way we handled ourselves in a particular moment that we shared with them. Then we ask them if they will return with us to that moment and replay it so that we can correct our actions or communication. A do-over is a replay of a real-life moment that corrects the mistakes of the moment in a real way. It's like a role-play with real-life consequences.

Kinetic Warm-Up: Play *Try Again*. Invite students to sit back-to-back on the floor. They will lean into each other and, without using their hands at all, use each other's weight to move from sitting on the floor to standing back-to-back.

Vocal Warm-Up: Invite students to sit in groups and complete the sentence, "I wish I had done _____ differently."

Conversation Starter Questions: We all have moments in our lives that we wish we had handled differently.

- What is one moment in your life that you wish you had handled differently?
- How might your relationship with the other people involved change if you ask them for a do-over?

Role-Play Ideas: Invite students to role-play a scenario where one friend [*gets mad at another/cancels plans with another/blames another for something they did not do*] and decides to ask for a do-over.

Freeze Ideas: Freeze the role-play at the point at which one character is confused by another character's request for a do-over. We may need to explain to others what we mean by "do-over."

- How would you explain the term "do-over" to someone who did not know what you meant?

Revise, Refine, Redo: Continue the role-play until the two characters have completed the role-play of the previously difficult moment in their lives.

- How can a do-over positively affect your relationships?
- What problems can a do-over solve that a simple apology may not be able to solve?

Everybody Practice: Invite students to work in pairs to role-play a moment between themselves and someone in their own lives from whom they would like to request a do-over. Encourage them to practice exactly what they would like to say and encourage them to prepare each other to use this technique on a real issue in their own lives.

Wrapping It Up—Synthesis Question:

- Do you feel prepared to use the do-over technique in your own life?

PARAPHRASING

Competency: Relationship Skills

Track: Listening to Our Minds

Definition: To paraphrase is to restate the meaning of a text or passage using other words. We can also paraphrase information that is shared with us verbally, such as someone else's point of view on a conflict or their personal story.

Detailed Description: We are all familiar with the skill of paraphrasing, which is often used in ELA classes when students are asked to restate the author's point of view in their own words. This academic style of paraphrasing is akin to a verbal summary of a written passage and often emphasizes the importance of restating the main idea of a passage in one or two sentences.

As a social and emotional learning skill, paraphrasing has a slightly different use, and for that reason we need a slightly different approach to this important skill. When we paraphrase someone's point of view on a story or conflict, we do it to demonstrate that we have listened deeply, understand their point of view, and want to help them feel better. When people are sharing their feelings, thoughts, or point of view on a story or conflict, they can easily feel disrespected if we reduce the details of their point of view to a one-sentence main idea. Therefore, we want to focus on capturing as many details as we can, because it is in the details of a story that the difficult emotions live.

Just imagine trying to explain to a close associate how someone cut you off in traffic. You probably would not take too kindly to them saying, "OK. I get it. You got cut off." But, if they carefully listen to the details of how this happened and then repeat that back to you faithfully, it is easy to imagine how this might assure you that your point of view was heard and respected.

Kinetic Warm-Up: Play *Handshakes*. Invite students to work in pairs. They will each develop a personal handshake/greeting made of a series of gestures. They will teach each other their handshakes/greetings and practice them until they have handshakes/greetings for both partners memorized. Invite all pairs to share with the larger group.

Vocal Warm-Up: In the same pairs, invite students to share a detail-rich story of what they did over the weekend. Encourage them to pack their story with details such as dates, times, locations, names, and how they were feeling. After the speaking partner shares their story, the listening partner will attempt to paraphrase and capture as many of the details as possible. The listening partner will then ask, "Did I get that right?" The speaking partner will then give the listening partner feedback about details that they missed. Reverse roles and repeat.

Conversation Starter Questions:

- How does it make you feel when someone listens to you carefully and captures all the details of your personal story?
- Why might we want to focus on and emphasize the details when we paraphrase someone else's point of view on a conflict or their story?
- How and why do the details of a personal story matter to the speaker?

Role-Play Ideas: Invite two students into the playing area to improvise a scenario between friends where one friend shares that they are upset because [*a teacher accused them of cheating/their father forgot their birthday/ another student made fun of their skin color/they were not invited to a party*]. Run the role-play once and have the character who is listening ignore the details and simply state the main idea.

Freeze Ideas: Freeze the role-play after the listening character has delivered their short, main idea paraphrase.

- What does the body language of these characters tell us about how they are feeling?

Revise, Refine, Redo: Redo the role-play and have the listening character focus on capturing all the details of the speaking character's story.

- How does deep listening change the way both characters are feeling?
- How do deep listening and detail-oriented paraphrasing change the relationship between the two characters?

Everybody Practice: Invite students to work in pairs. This time they will share a story of an important event in their life. It could be a positive event or a more difficult event. Each partner will attempt to listen deeply, capture all the important details of the story and the speaker's feelings, and paraphrase the story. They will then say, "Did I get that right?" and the speaker will give them feedback on any important details that they missed. Reverse roles and repeat.

Wrapping It Up—Synthesis Questions:

- How did it feel when your partner tried to listen deeply and capture all the details of your personal story?
- When do you think it might be helpful to listen deeply and paraphrase the details of someone's story?

- Is there someone in your life for whom you would like to listen deeply and paraphrase?

POSITIVE AFFIRMATIONS

Competency: Relationship Skills

Track: Listening to Our Emotions

Definition: A positive affirmation is a statement that defines and confirms something positive about a person or situation.

Detailed Description: We all appreciate when someone affirms something positive about us. Positive affirmations from others often make us realize the positive effect we have on others, help us to appreciate our own talents, and strengthen our relationships. In addition, we can consciously decide, through the use of positive self-talk, to give ourselves positive affirmations. These positive affirmations that come from us and are delivered to us often help us to bolster our own confidence, reconnect to our own motivations, and be calm and patient in difficult situations.

The key to creating powerful positive affirmations is to make sure that we are acknowledging the deeper personal qualities of those we are talking to, be that others or ourselves. In our culture, where both adults and young people are more comfortable with surface affirmations—for instance, about what someone has or how they look—giving positive affirmations that acknowledge someone's behavior, talents, potential, or personality traits is often a new skill.

Kinetic Warm-Up: Play *High Five*. Invite students to stand in a circle and pass a high five around the circle. Then invite students to create their own unique and more elaborate version of a high five. Each student will share their unique high five with the person to their right. That person will learn and repeat it, and return it back to them. Then that person will share their own unique high five with the person to their right.

Vocal Warm-Up: Invite students to work in groups and brainstorm positive affirmations that acknowledge behavior, talents, potential, or personality traits and that they could share with a classmate, family member, or friend.

Conversation Starter Questions: Sometimes it is difficult to think of what we might want to share in a positive affirmation, even if we have positive thoughts and feelings about someone else. It can be even harder if we have negative thoughts and feelings about someone, even though we can usually find something positive to affirm in everyone. If you are struggling to come up with a positive affirmation for someone, you might ask yourself these questions:

- What is something your classmate, family member, or friend does that you wish you could do?

- What is something that your classmate, family member, or friend does that helps others?
- What is one of your classmate's, family member's, or friend's positive personal qualities?

Role-Play Ideas: Invite two students to improvise a scenario where one character is feeling defeated after [*being told that they will move next year/being told their work will not be shown in an art exhibit/being ignored by their friend group*] and the other character offers positive affirmations to help them feel better.

Freeze Ideas: Freeze the scene after the defeated character has received at least two positive affirmations.

- What feeling(s) is their face and body language expressing now?
- What effect can positive affirmations have on someone who is feeling defeated?

Revise, Refine, Redo: Redo the role-play and have the defeated character use positive affirmations with themselves. In this role-play, the defeated character will write in a journal and verbally speak the positive affirmations that they write to and about themselves.

Everybody Practice: Invite students to partner with someone they do not know well. Ask them to take a moment to think about that person. Even if they do not know them well, being in class with each other means that they have some information about each other even if they are not close. Invite each student to share at least two positive affirmations about their partner's behavior, talents, potential, or personal qualities.

Wrapping It Up—Synthesis Questions: Positive affirmations can completely alter our mood, change our point of view on a situation, and deepen our relationships.

- Do you have a classmate, family member, or friend to whom you would like to give a positive affirmation?
- What behavior, talent, potential, or personal quality would you like to affirm?
- How could you use positive affirmations in your self-talk to help change your mood or boost your own confidence?

EMOTIONAL EMPATHY

Competency: Relationship Skills

Track: Listening to Our Emotions

Definition: Empathy is the ability to understand and share the feelings of another.

Detailed Description: Empathy is often presented as a personal quality that some of us have and others don't. But we can also look at empathy as a set of related skills that we can all develop. Social scientists suggest that there are three different types of empathy: cognitive, emotional, and compassionate.

Emotional empathy is the ability to share in someone else's emotion, or to feel what they are feeling as they are feeling it. We do not have to share identical experiences with another person in order to feel emotional empathy for them. If we can identify the emotions that their experiences inspire, we can identify a time in our own lives when we had similar emotions. Even if the actual events in our lives were very different, we can always identify a time that we experienced similar emotions.

But, sometimes emotional empathy is a challenge because we choose to deny, forget, or minimize our own difficult experiences as a way of coping with them. In order to express emotional empathy, we need to be willing to admit our struggles and see them as a valuable asset in understanding and connecting with others.

Kinetic Warm-Up: Play *Pass an Emotion*. Invite students to stand in a circle. Name an emotion (e.g., confused, angry, joyful) and invite students to make a facial expression and movement that expresses this emotion. They will pass the emotional movement to the person to their right. That person will receive it, repeat it, and then pass their own emotional movement to the person to their right.

Vocal Warm-Up: Invite students to work in groups. Invite them to share stories that made them joyful and have them take note that, although the stories vary widely, the emotion is the same. Invite them to share stories that made them angry and have them take note that, although the stories vary widely, the emotion is the same.

Conversation Starter Questions: One of the things that prevents us from expressing emotional empathy is our own embarrassment about our experiences, our feelings, or our own struggles. We often think that experiences of struggle make us appear weak to others. But seeing our struggles as the growth opportunities that they are is a special kind of strength.

- Why do you feel uncomfortable admitting or sharing your emotions or struggles with others, if you do?
- How might your ability to be comfortable with your own struggles benefit you and others?

Role-Play Ideas: Invite two students into the playing area and have them improvise a scenario where one character is feeling defeated after [*being told that they will move next year/being made fun of for their accent/being told their work will not be shown in an art exhibit/being ignored by their friend group*]. The other character identifies and shares a time in their life where they had similar emotions and expresses that they understand what the speaker is feeling now.

Freeze Ideas: Freeze the scene after the listening character has shared their story of struggle and both characters are equally vulnerable.

- What do you notice about the facial expressions and body language of the two characters?
- How does expressing emotional empathy deepen the connection between people?

Revise, Refine, Redo: Allow the scenario to play out.

- How does the character who is currently despondent feel after the listening character shares in that emotion?

Redo the role-play and have the listening character refuse to express emotional empathy by saying something like, "That must be hard" or "I can't relate; that has never happened to me."

- How does the refusal to express emotional empathy affect the relationship between the two characters?

Everybody Practice: Invite students to work in pairs. Have them share a story from their own lives that was difficult for them and ask them to share the emotions that it inspired. Invite their partner to think of an experience in their own life in which they experienced the same emotion. Ask them to share the experience and express that they can understand why and how their partner felt the way they did. Reverse roles and repeat.

Wrapping It Up—Synthesis Questions: When we want to express emotional empathy, we need to build a bridge between someone else's experiences and our own. We can do that by listening carefully and asking ourselves these questions:

- Have I ever felt as [*angry/scared/joyful*] as the speaker?
- How did my emotion feel inside my body at that time?

- Can I remember that same emotion and feel it now?

"I FEEL" MESSAGES

Competency: Relationships Skills

Track: Listening to Our Emotions

Definition: "I feel" messages communicate our feelings without assigning blame.

Detailed Description: When we are experiencing difficult feelings, we have a tendency to blame those we are close to for causing these feelings within us. We may use accusatory statements such as "It's all your fault!" or "You made me yell because you keep pushing me for an answer." When we indirectly express our feelings through accusations, we often cause other problems, including a missed opportunity to express the true cause of our feelings, and a defensive response from the receiver of our accusation.

"I feel" messages can help us to more clearly communicate our feelings and in a way that others can listen and respond to positively and productively. "I feel" messages are best delivered to people who know us well, care about us, and want to protect our relationship. They are not very effective with people who do not know us, do not care about us, and with whom we have no meaningful relationship. The simple form of an "I feel" message is as follows:

I feel [*describe your emotion*]
when [*describe the situation*]
because I [*describe the reasons for your response*].

Kinetic Warm-Up: Play *In My Feelings*. Invite students to work in groups and make feelings tableaus that then they present to the larger group.

Vocal Warm-Up: Set a timer for three minutes. In the same groups, invite students to brainstorm as many feeling words as they can and chart them. Share the charts from all groups.

Conversation Starter Questions: Accusations of any kind usually stop communication, as both people often become increasingly defensive. It is very common that people respond to an accusation with a denial, and this common response doesn't change much with age or maturity. A kindergartener who says to their peer, "You stole my marker!" often hears, "No, I didn't!" as a response. A college student who says to their roommate, "It was your turn to do the dishes" often hears, "No, it wasn't" as a response. And, a spouse who says to their partner, "You hurt my feelings" often hears, "You're misinterpreting me" as a response.

Accusations are simply not a very effective communication tool, as communication often breaks down after an accusation is delivered. Practice creating some "I feel" messages that could be delivered in real-life situations and pay attention to the tendency that people have of turning an "I feel" message into an accusation. For instance, "I feel mad when you take my marker because you always do that!" This statement is not an "I feel" message at all, but an accusation. As the accusative voice often leads us toward creating statements of blame, the use of the word "you" in the second line of an "I feel" message can easily trip anyone up.

One way to make sure that our "I feel" message *truly* conveys the feeling, describes the situation, and explains the impact of the behavior is by removing the "you" in the second line. A simple way to make this adjustment is to replace the word "you" with words like "anyone," "someone," "my friends," "people I am close to," or "my family."

Role-Play Ideas: Invite two students to improvise a scenario where one character accuses another of [*interrupting them in a conversation/making fun of their ethnic background/making fun of their accent/stealing their idea*].

Freeze Ideas: Freeze the scenario after the accusation has been delivered.

- What do the facial expressions and body language of these two characters tell you about how they are feeling?

Revise, Refine, Redo: Redo the role-play and have the character deliver an "I feel" message instead.

- How does the body language of the two characters change?
- How does an "I feel" message improve communication in general?

Everybody Practice: Invite students to work in groups and share situations that are currently bothering them. Could an "I feel" message help? Have students work together and help one another construct effective "I feel" messages that they can deliver to people in their own lives.

Wrapping It Up—Synthesis Questions: In our personal relationships, it is helpful if we avoid using accusations to communicate our feelings and instead use "I feel" messages.

- Did you craft an "I feel" message in your group that you will deliver to someone in your life?
- Does anyone need more help crafting an effective "I feel" message?

PASSIVE, ASSERTIVE, AGGRESSIVE COMMUNICATION

Competency: Relationship Skills

Track: Listening to Our Environment

Definition: *Passive communication* involves "giving in" to a directly stated or implied threat and doing something against your own better judgment. *Assertive communication* involves laying down boundaries and doing what you believe is right without threatening or hurting others. *Aggressive communication* uses personal, social, or physical threats to bend or force others to adopt your point of view or actions.

Detailed Description: We all are faced with people in our lives who have a tendency to dominate others with aggressive communication. The domination often takes the form of a direct or indirect threat that is either personal (a threat to hurt someone's feelings or relationships), social (a threat to hurt someone's reputation), or physical (a threat to hurt someone's body). In response, we may return the aggressive communication by making threats ourselves. We may be passive by giving into others' threats, or we might be assertive by laying down boundaries and standing up for ourselves without hurting or threatening others. Being assertive is usually the best choice, although it may not be the easiest choice.

Kinetic Warm-Up: Invite students to work in small groups to make physical tableaus that illustrate aggressive communication, passive communication, and assertive communication. Pay attention the way the body language in each tableau differs.

Vocal Warm-Up: In the same small groups invite students to brainstorm statements that would be examples of aggressive communication, passive communication, and assertive communication. Pay attention to the defining factor of the embedded threat for aggressive communication, the sense of "giving in" or "giving up" in passive communication, and the sense of clear boundaries and a respect for self and others in assertive communication.

Conversation Starter Questions: We have already learned some assertive communication techniques including the power of saying no, defining personal space, remaining neutral, asking for thinking time, initiating do-overs, practicing self-talk, and crafting "I feel" statements.

- Can you think of some other ways that you could communicate assertively in the face of someone else's aggression?

One simple and powerful assertive communication technique is when we "name the game" by simply letting people know that we see what they are doing and it does not affect us. For instance:

- Aggressive communication, personal threat: *If you don't let me copy your test answers, I'm not going to hang out with you.*
- Assertive communication, "name the game": *I hear that you are giving me a threat, but it does not affect me. You are not copying my answers.*

Another assertive communication technique, called "I'm outta here," is to simply leave the conversation when someone insists on being aggressive. When you use this technique, you say what you have to say and then leave. You break the unhealthy connection.

- Aggressive communication, social threat: *Everyone thinks you look really dumb in that shirt.*
- Assertive communication "I'm outta here": *I don't think so. Bye.*

Role-Play Ideas: Invite students to role-play a scenario where one character threatens another by saying [*they will tell everyone at school that his or her family is illegal/other kids won't want to date him or her because of their color/that they want to fight after school*].

Freeze Ideas: Role-play each scenario first with a passive response. Then try any one of the assertive responses that have been learned previously or are mentioned in this lesson. Freeze the scene after the passive message has been delivered.

- How do you think the person who delivered the passive message is feeling?

Freeze the scene after the assertive message has been delivered.

- How do you think the person who delivered the assertive message is feeling?

Revise, Refine, Redo: Redo each scenario and explore what happens when both people are aggressive.

Everybody Practice: Invite students to work in pairs and share a time when someone was communicating aggressively with them. What assertive communication technique could they have used? Could they ask for a do-over with that person and communicate with them assertively now?

Wrapping It Up—Synthesis Question: Assertive communication is difficult because it requires us to respect ourselves and others, even if we are upset.

- Is there someone with whom you often communicate aggressively and would now like to communicate assertively?

SAFE WAYS TO BE AN ALLY

Competency: Responsible Decision-Making

Track: Listening to Our Bodies

Definition: An ally is someone who positions themselves to help, provide assistance, and support others in an ongoing effort, activity, or struggle.

Detailed Description: All of us need allies. In many situations, being an ally simply requires our time and a generosity of spirit that allows us to extend a helping hand to others. But, in some cases we might want to help someone who is in some kind of danger. They may be the target of a bully, who uses their perceived power to threaten others, or the target of prejudice or discrimination. In these situations, we need to weigh whether it is best to confront the aggressor with assertive language or to safely remove the person being targeted and ourselves.

People who are committed to aggressive communication and aggressive action are often unreceptive to assertive messages or may interpret them as aggression. So, in extreme cases of bullying, prejudice, and discrimination it is sometimes better to be an ally by providing a safe way out of the situation.

Kinetic Warm-Up: Play *Safety in Numbers*. Invite students to stand in a circle and link hands with the person one person away from them. This will result in a lattice of linked hands in front of all the participants. Then invite everyone to carefully lift their linked hands out in front of them, above their heads, and behind their backs. This will result in an all-encompassing "group hug" with all participants' hands linked behind their backs.

Vocal Warm-Up: Invite students to talk in small groups and respond to the prompt "I feel safe when . . ."

Conversation Starter Questions: Many of history's greatest tragedies unfolded under the watchful eye of passive bystanders. In fact, the more bystanders there are, the less likely it is that any of them will help—a phenomenon called the "bystander effect." Sometimes bystanders presume that the issue is a personal one between the aggressor and targeted person and they "don't want to get involved." Sometimes they believe that the targeted person must have done something to deserve the harsh treatment of the aggressor. Sometimes they have underlying biases that allow them to feel separate from the targeted person. But perhaps the most powerful reason, and one that may underlie all the others, is that the bystanders are simply afraid.

Many of us believe that if we move from being a passive bystander to being an active ally, we must engage directly with the aggressor. We fear that the aggressor will turn on us, and we will become the targeted person.

- Have you ever watched someone who is the target of bullying, prejudice, or discrimination and done nothing at all?
- Why did you decide to remain a bystander at that time?

Role-Play Ideas: Invite students into the playing area and ask them to improvise a scenario where someone is being targeted for [*the color of their skin/the language they speak/the way they dress/the shape or size of their body/ their learning style*]. Invite students to practice this simple assertiveness technique called the "Join Me/Us" Intervention:

1. Approach the situation, smile, and make eye contact with the targeted person. Stand behind or to the side of the aggressor so that the targeted person can easily see you want to help.
2. Maintain that eye contact and say something like, "Hi, [*target's name*]. It's great to see you. I'm going to [*eat/play basketball/study*]. Come join me!"
3. Don't engage with or respond to the aggressor. Even if they ask you direct questions, simply ignore them by maintaining your eye contact with the targeted person.
4. If it's appropriate, you can move to stand next to them and repeat the same invitation. Continue to maintain your eye contact with the target. Don't engage with the aggressor.
5. Walk away from the aggressor together and make sure the targeted person is safe. Invite them to join you in doing whatever you planned, if possible.

Freeze Ideas: Freeze the role-play at each step and check that the ally is making eye contact with the targeted person. Analyze how everyone's body language changes throughout.

Revise, Refine, Redo: Repeat with multiple scenarios. Invite students to find ally partners. Redo without the use of the "Join Me/Us" Intervention.

- How do bystanders end up hurting others?

Everybody Practice: Invite students to practice the "Join Me/Us" Intervention in small groups.

Wrapping It Up—Synthesis Question: Being an ally takes courage. It can be easier with this intervention and even easier if we find partners who will act as allies with us.

- What fears do you still have about being an ally?

IDENTIFYING UNDERLYING CAUSES

Competency: Responsible Decision-Making

Track: Listening to Our Minds

Definition: Underlying causes are the unique, often ignored, root causes of a problem or conflict.

Detailed Description: Conflict, struggles, and other problems can be uncomfortable. When we encounter conflict, struggles, or other problems we want to solve them as quickly as possible. But, in our effort to resolve things quickly, we often ignore an important process of rooting out and uncovering the underlying causes of the problem. When we ignore this process, we often decide on solutions that are not very effective because they do not address the root cause of the problem. So, we need to make it a practice, when we are faced with struggles of any kind, to search for the root causes of the problem before generating solutions. This will ensure that we decide on a solution that actually addresses the root causes and will therefore be more likely to be effective.

Kinetic Warm-Up: Play *Make It Work*. Invite students to stand in a circle. They will pass an object (book, coin, marker) around the circle without using their hands. They must not drop it when passing it from one person to the next.

Vocal Warm-Up: Invite students to talk in groups about solutions to various problems in their own lives that have not been effective. Ask them to discuss why these solutions were ineffective.

Conversation Starter Questions: We all have experienced someone offering a hasty solution to a problem that we knew would not work. Maybe a parent got lost while driving somewhere and decided to use their instincts to return to the correct route rather than identifying where and how they made the wrong turn. Maybe we had trouble after studying diligently for a test and were told to "study harder" without any input as to how we might improve our study techniques. Maybe we were punished for having a fight with our sibling without anyone bothering to discover what the fight was actually about.

We likely knew that none of these hasty solutions solved the problem, and we may have discovered that, in fact, they made it worse. In each of these examples, the people involved failed to ask themselves and each other the essential question, "Why is this happening?" When we have struggles of any kind, if we can develop a habit of asking ourselves why things have occurred in the way they have, we will have a better chance of generating an effective solution.

- What do you think prevents people from asking themselves and others the essential question, "Why is this happening?"
- What do you think prevents people from exploring the underlying causes of a problem?

Role-Play Ideas: Invite students into the playing area to improvise a scenario where [*a parent gets lost while driving/a student gets a low mark on a test after studying/two siblings get punished after fighting*]. Run the role-play once where no one asks, "Why is this happening?" and observe how the problem actually gets worse even though a solution is applied. Then run the role-play where characters ask the essential question and observe what solution they decide upon.

Freeze Ideas: Freeze the action as the problem is escalating, even though a solution has been applied.

- What does the body language of each character tell us about how they are feeling?

Freeze the action after the essential question has been asked by one of the characters.

- What does the body language tell us about how the characters are feeling at this moment?

Revise, Refine, Redo: Allow the scenario to play out to completion after the essential question has been asked. Push the characters to explore all the possible underlying causes and remind them that there are often many.

- Do you think the solution that the characters came up with will be effective?
- Does the solution that the characters came up with actually address one of the strongest underlying causes of the problem?

Everybody Practice: Invite students to work in pairs and share problems that they are experiencing in their lives presently. Invite one partner to share the problem and have the other partner paraphrase what was shared and then ask the essential question, "Why do you think this is happening?" Push students to explore all the possible reasons that this struggle or problem might be presenting itself. Then see if they can come up with a solution that addresses the strongest underlying cause of the problem. Switch roles and repeat.

Wrapping It Up—Synthesis Question: If we can get in the habit of asking the essential question "Why is this happening?" when we are presented with any kind of struggle, we will have a chance to create an effective solution.

- How can you bring this idea of exploring underlying causes to problems that you are experiencing in your own friend circle or family?

WANTS, NEEDS, AND PRIORITIES

Competency: Responsible Decision-Making

Track: Listening to Our Minds

Definition: A *need* is a thing, a circumstance, an interaction, or a relationship that is important and essential. A *want* is a thing, a circumstance, an interaction, or a relationship that you wish for or desire.

Detailed Description: We all share the need for food, clothing, and shelter. But we have other basic needs, such as the emotional needs we discussed previously or the need for time to accomplish our goals and fulfill our responsibilities. We all have wants, or things that are not essential but that we feel will bring us joy or pleasure. While it could be argued that joy and pleasure, which often come from our wants, are actually essential needs, it's also true that just because we really want something does not mean that we need it.

What can be challenging is finding the balance between our wants and our needs. This involves allotting our resources (our energy, time, money) in a thoughtful way. If we can balance our wants and needs, thoughtfully allocate the resources we have, and prioritize intelligently, we may be able to do/get both what we want and what we need.

Kinetic Warm-Up: Play *I Want*. Form a circle of chairs with one fewer chair than the number of participants. Ask all but one student to sit in a chair and ask the lone student to stand in the middle of the circle. Invite them to make a statement using this formula: "Everyone who wants _____, go find it!" Any student who shares the want that is expressed in the statement will move to change their seat. The student left without a seat will stand in the middle and make a new statement using the same formula.

Vocal Warm-Up: Invite students to work in groups and brainstorm a list of wants and needs. Invite each group to share their list with the larger group.

Conversation Starter Questions: Many of us struggle with balancing our wants and our needs. If we prioritize our wants over our needs, we may put ourselves in a position of failing to meet our goals or fulfill our responsibilities. The questions that we always need to ask ourselves when we are thinking about pursuing a want versus a need are:

- Do I have the resources (energy, time, money) available to pursue what I want?
- Will I still be able to meet my goals and fulfill my responsibilities if I prioritize my wants over my needs?

- "Have I ever prioritized a want and then failed to meet a goal or fulfill my responsibilities?"

Role-Play Ideas: Invite two students to improvise a scene where one character invites another to [*blow off studying to go ride bikes/leave his or her chores for the next day/play video games instead of help cook dinner*]. The character being invited will ask for thinking time and then will use self-talk to ask themselves the essential questions, "Do I have the time?" and "Will I still be able to fulfill by responsibilities?"

Freeze Ideas: Freeze the scene after the character being invited has asked for thinking time. Invite the audience to partner with this character, while the other character is still frozen, to answer the essential questions in their self-talk. Once this character has made a good decision, unfreeze and let them communicate their decision.

Revise, Refine, Redo: Allow the scenario to play out and observe what happens if the first character tries to pressure the second to go back on their good decision.

- How might we need to use assertive communication when we are pressured to make a bad decision?

Redo the scenario and examine what happens if both characters favor their wants over their needs.

- What kind of problems does favoring wants over needs create for both characters?

Everybody Practice: Invite students to work in small groups and talk about the things they really want to do with their time and the things they need to do with their time. Ask them to strategize ways to use their time that allows them to both fulfill their responsibilities and do some of what they want to do.

Wrapping It Up—Synthesis Question: Throughout our lives, we will need to balance our wants and our needs. We will always need to think about the resources we have (energy, time, money) and intelligently allocate them so that we prioritize what we need to do, but always have the chance to do what we want as well.

- What do you think is the best way to make sure you fulfill your responsibilities but also can do some of what you want?

COMPASSIONATE EMPATHY

Competency: Responsible Decision-Making

Track: Listening to Our Emotions

Definition: Empathy is the ability to understand and share the feelings of another.

Detailed Description: Empathy is often presented as a personal quality that some of us have and others don't. But we can also look at empathy as a set of related skills that we can all develop. Social scientists suggest that there are three different types of empathy: cognitive, emotional, and compassionate.

Compassionate empathy is the ability to integrate cognitive and emotional empathy and take appropriate action to help someone change their situation and feel better. Unlike cognitive empathy and emotional empathy, compassionate empathy involves actually doing something to help change someone else's situation for the better. For this reason, it can be the most challenging type of empathy to express; it requires that we step out of our comfort zone and put someone else's emotional needs ahead of our own.

Kinetic Warm-Up: Play *Trust Fall*. This common exercise is a great way to physically communicate the idea that we are all dependent on the kindness of others at one point or another. Have students work in groups of at least seven. One participant will stand with their back to the group members and gently lean and fall into their hands. Repeat until all group members have had a chance to trust their group to catch them.

Vocal Warm-Up: In the same small groups, ask students to talk about a time they truly needed help from someone else and received it, a time they helped someone else who needed it, and a time they knew someone needed help but they denied it.

Conversation Starter Questions: Sometimes we see the neediness or powerlessness of others as a sign of their weakness or their mistakes. Rather than opening ourselves to the pain that others might be feeling, we may secretly stand in judgment of their pain and actually blame them for it. This is common with people we assume to be poor—for instance, the homeless. We may walk by them on the street and make comments about how they look or smell. But, this resistance to expressing compassionate empathy is a reflection of something within the person who judges others, not an accurate reflection of the person whom they are judging.

- Why do you think we sometimes judge others who are struggling rather than expressing compassionate empathy through the effort to help them?

Role-Play Ideas: Invite a group of students into the playing area and ask them to improvise a scenario where a homeless person is asking for change or food. In the first version, have the group of students ignore the homeless person and say demeaning things about them. In a second version, have one member of the student group practice cognitive empathy by listening carefully to their story, emotional empathy by simply remembering a time when they too were hungry, and compassionate empathy by offering to help by sharing food or change.

Freeze Ideas: Freeze the first role-play when all the students are making fun of the homeless person.

- What do the facial expressions and body language tell you about what the student group is feeling and thinking?
- What does the facial expression and body language of the homeless person tell you about what they are feeling and thinking?

Freeze the second role-play after one member of the student group decides to engage the homeless person.

- How do the other students react?
- What does this reaction tell us about their thoughts and feelings?

Revise, Refine, Redo: Redo the role-play and explore what happens if all the members of the student group talk about how they might be able to help, rather than making fun of the homeless person.

Everybody Practice: Invite students to work in pairs. They will each share something with which they could use some help. Their partner will listen deeply, paraphrase their point of view, and reflect their feelings (cognitive empathy). They will then identify a time in their own life when they had similar feelings (emotional empathy). Lastly, they will offer some help to their partner (compassionate empathy). Reverse roles and repeat.

Wrapping It Up—Synthesis Questions: Compassionate empathy can be the most challenging type of empathy to express because it requires us to leave the comfort zone of our own environment and put someone else's needs before our own.

- Is there someone in your life to whom you would like to express compassionate empathy?
- What would you like to do to help carry their load?

"I NEED" MESSAGES

Competency: Responsible Decision-Making

Track: Listening to Our Emotions

Definition: An "I need" message is a simple and direct way to be assertive and get our needs met, even with people we don't know well.

Detailed Description: An "I feel" message is a staple of social and emotional learning that allows us to be assertive when we're upset about something another person has done. But, an "I feel" message is best used with people who know us, care about us, and have time to engage with us.

When we try to use "I feel" messages with people who don't have a vested interest in us, or who simply don't have time to engage, the message can actually backfire. Imagine a third-grader giving a sixth-grader an "I feel" message about being left out of a basketball game. The game would need to come to a halt, the sixth-graders would need to turn their attention to listening to the feelings of someone who is not a peer, and from there it is hard to say what would happen.

Or imagine using an "I feel" message when a classmate has skipped you in line. The whole line might move on before the message had been delivered and received. In situations where there is not a lot of time and where the message that has to be delivered is more practical than personal, "I need" messages can be the better choice. An "I need" message is a short and sweet way of being assertive and getting your needs met. It doesn't ask the receiver for verbal engagement but for action.

Kinetic Warm-Up: Play *Can You Move?* Invite students to lead one another in a series of physical movements. The leader will call out, "Can you do three jumping jacks, four sit-ups, and five long, deep breaths?" Invite different students to lead.

Vocal Warm-Up: Invite students to work in small groups and brainstorm situations when an "I need" message might be a better choice than an "I feel" message. Encourage them to think about situations where they have to work with others who they may not know well, or where the information that they have to convey is time sensitive and practical rather than personal.

Conversation Starter Questions: To form an "I need" message, simply state your needs and end with an expression of thanks. Sometimes identifying and valuing our needs can be difficult. We might imagine that the needs of others are more important than our own, and decide not to communicate our needs at all. Or we might imagine that we will be met with resistance if we communicate our needs and end up stating them in the form of an accusation, such as "You are rushing me!" or "You're so loud!" But by learning and practicing "I need" messages, such as "I need more time. Thanks!" or "I need some quiet to concentrate. Thanks!" we can begin making assertive rather than accusative statements that help us get our needs met.

- Can you think of a time when you made an accusation in an attempt to get your needs met? How did this go?

Role-Play Ideas: Invite a group of students to improvise a scenario in which their characters are working on a group project and one of the participants is dominating the conversation. The other characters can practice giving "I need" messages in which they express their need to have a chance to speak.

Freeze Ideas: Freeze the role-play after an "I need" message has been delivered.

- What do the body language and facial expressions of the participants tell us about how they are feeling?

Revise, Refine, Redo: Replay the same scenarios where no one conveys their needs to speak or contribute.

- How does this affect the overall collaboration and the relationships in the group?

Everybody Practice: Invite students to work in pairs and brainstorm "I need" messages that they would like to give to people in their own lives.

Wrapping It Up—Synthesis Question: "I need" messages are a simple and direct way to get our practical needs met, but they do require some courage.

- What fears do you have about delivering an "I need" message?

MEDIATION

Competency: Responsible Decision-Making

Track: Listening to Our Environment

Definition: Mediation is an interactive process in which a neutral third party assists disputing parties in resolving conflict through listening, paraphrasing, reflecting feelings, and creative questioning.

Detailed Description: Sometimes when two or more people are in conflict, it can help to have a third person assist them in coming to a resolution. This third person is a mediator. Professional mediators all share some of the same skills, which include the ability to remain neutral, listen deeply, and accurately paraphrase; a commitment to keep their own ideas to themselves; a commitment to encourage the people in conflict to come up with their own ideas for solutions; and some creative questioning skills to use when people get stuck. While these skills are used by professionals, we can use them in our own lives to help our classmates, friends, and families find lasting resolutions to their own problems.

Kinetic Warm-Up: Play *Ball Toss*. Invite students to stand in a circle. Using a small, soft ball (pom-pom, Koosh ball), ask one student to start by calling out another student's name and passing the ball across the circle to that person. The second student will pass it to a third, and so on, until all students have thrown and received the ball. Then invite them to repeat the same pattern without using their voices to call out each other's names. Give them all a chance to reconfirm who they received the ball from and who they passed it to. Then let them try to repeat the pattern. If they succeed, add another ball into the mix midway through to increase the challenge.

Vocal Warm-Up: We all have someone in our lives who likely serves as a mediator. It may be a parent, a teacher, a coach, or a good friend who seems to have a talent for listening to both sides of a disagreement and helping us to find a resolution.

- Who in your life seems to have some mediation skills already?
- How have they helped you to work out your problems peacefully?

Conversation Starter Questions: Mediation involves integrating the skills of neutrality, deep listening, paraphrasing, and reflecting feelings to help others find a resolution to their problems. If two or more people are having a conflict but they all want to work out a solution, we can informally mediate by simply sitting with them in a quiet space, listening to each of them individually tell their side of the story, paraphrasing what they share, and asking some questions to help them find a resolution that works for all of them.

Sometimes people interrupt one another, and we may need to remind them that we want to hear each of them without interruption. And sometimes people have trouble coming up with their own resolutions, so we will need to ask them some questions to help.

- What questions could you ask people in conflict that would help them find their own resolution?

Role-Play Ideas: Invite three students into the paying area to improvise a scenario where [*one friend called another a "homo"/one friend borrowed another friend's clothes and never returned them/one friend made fun of another's learning style/one friend started going out with another's ex-boyfriend or ex-girlfriend*]. One student will play the mediator and will approach the two friends who are fighting to see if they want help working out their disagreement peacefully.

The mediator should listen to both sides of the story, paraphrase, and reflect their feelings. Then they can ask these questions to each character individually, and paraphrase each answer.

- Do you understand how the other person is feeling?
- What do you need from the other person in order to feel better and move on?
- What could you do now to make this situation better?
- Can you agree to give each other what you need to feel better and move on?

Freeze Ideas: Mediation is both simple and very difficult. In the simplest sense, it is about listening, paraphrasing, and reflecting back people's points of view and feelings. But it can get complicated because it may be hard to stay neutral and people may have a lot to say. Freeze the role-play at all the different stages of the mediation and ask the audience to help the mediator, or switch out the mediator for a new student actor who will pick up where the scene left off.

Revise, Refine, Redo: Redo with a different conflict and different student actors.

Everybody Practice: Have students work in groups of three and improvise a mediation scenario of their choice. Give students enough time to work through all the parts of a mediation: listening, paraphrasing, reflecting feelings, asking questions. Invite all groups to share the conflict or problem they explored and the resolution they settled upon.

Wrapping It Up—Synthesis Question:

- How and when could you use mediation skills in your own life?

STANDING UP TO OPPRESSION

Competency: Responsible Decision-Making

Track: Listening to Our Environment

Definition: Oppression involves the favoring of one social group over another by people, groups, or institutions that hold power. Oppression is maintained through social norms, stereotypes, biases, prejudices, discrimination, and institutional rules.

Detailed Description: In general terms, oppression describes a situation where those in power use bias, stereotypes, prejudice, discrimination, and other privileges of their position to deny rights, respect, and access to opportunity to those with less power. In history class, we may have learned about authoritarian regimes where the government exerts extreme control, which can be violent, over its citizens. But oppression may not be as direct as this example.

We may notice that some people in our community are afforded opportunities that others of us are not. We may experience people in power using stereotypes to describe us. We may experience people in power acting with prejudice or discrimination against others in our own community. It can be challenging to know what to do when we face oppression within our own community, but there are way to address it.

- Describe a time you witnessed someone in power expressing bias or using a stereotype. How did you feel?
- What, if anything, did you do in response at the time?

Kinetic Warm-Up: Play *Power Tableaus*. Invite students to work in small groups and create tableaus that depict one group exerting power over another group. They might have physical power or status, social power, economic power, or psychological power.

Vocal Warm-Up: In the same groups ask students to share their ideas based on this prompt: "It's not fair when _____."

Conversation Starter Questions: When we are faced with oppression of some kind, we often respond with silence. We may see a large group of boys taunting a girl, we may see a teacher insulting a student's intelligence, we may see a principal calling one group of kids "good kids" and another group "bad kids" and notice that each of those groups comprises kids who have the same ethnicity.

When people, groups, or institutions with power act in ways that are oppressive, it sends a very strong message to everyone else in that community, saying, "Stay in the place we have put you or there may be more trouble for you." So, we may become silent and think about how to keep ourselves safe. But, if we talk to one another about what we have witnessed and experienced, and if we join together as allies, we can fight oppression in our communities. Because people, groups, and institutions that oppress others have some type of power, it is important to protect yourself when confronting them by always seeking allies, communicating assertively and peacefully, and keeping everyone safe. These allies may be your peers or they may be adults.

Role-Play Ideas: Invite a group of students to improvise a scene where a police officer sees a group of students outside of a store on a public bench after school and says something like, "What are you doing here? You can't hang out here. Get out of here!" Part 1 of the scene should explore why the students believe that the police officer is denying them the right to sit together on a public bench. Is it their color, their class, their gender? Part 2 could explore who the students believe could join them as allies and what action they could take that would safely fight the oppression they experienced.

Freeze Ideas: Freeze the scene in Part 1 as the students are talking about why they believe the police officer is denying them their rights. Ask the audience for ideas. Freeze Part 2 as the group and their allies are thinking about how they can safely fight the oppression. There is no one right answer or one right way to fight oppression. But, it is always important to work with your allies, communicate assertively and peacefully, and keep everyone safe.

Revise, Refine, Redo: Explore another situation, such as a group of boys denying a girl the right to play basketball.

- Who will her allies be?
- What kind of assertive and peaceful action can they take together to fight the oppression the boys are enacting on the female athlete?

Everybody Practice: Invite students to talk in groups about who their adult allies are and what kinds of assertive and peaceful communication could help fight oppression (e.g., letters, peaceful demonstrations, mediations, rallies).

Wrapping It Up—Synthesis Question: Standing up to oppression is complicated and challenging, but our country is built on people standing up peacefully for their rights and the rights of others.

- What examples from history inspire you to fight oppression in your lives today?

References

CHAPTER 1

Aristotle. *The Nicomachean Ethics*. 2nd ed. New York, NY: Oxford University Press, 2009.
Collaborative for Academic, Social, and Emotional Learning. "Core SEL Competencies." https://casel.org/core-competencies.
Ericsson, Anders, and Robert Pool. *PEAK: Secrets from the New Science of Expertise*. New York, NY: Eamon Dolan/Mariner Books, 2017.
Goleman, Daniel. *Emotional Intelligence: Why It Can Matter More Than IQ*. New York, NY: Bantam Books, 1995.
Kolb, David A. *Experiential Learning: Experience as the Source of Learning and Development*. Upper Saddle River, NJ: Prentice Hall, 1984.
Pink, Daniel H. *Drive: The Surprising Truth about What Motivates Us*. New York, NY: Riverhead Books, 2011.
Salovey, Peter, and John D. Mayer. "Emotional Intelligence." *Imagination, Cognition, and Personality* 9, no. 3 (1990): 185–211. https://doi.org/10.2190/DUGG-P24E-52WK-6CDG.

CHAPTER 2

Iacoboni, Marco. *Mirroring People: The Science of Empathy and How We Connect with Others*. New York, NY: Farrar, Straus and Giroux, 2008.
Tomlinson, Carol Ann. *The Differentiated Classroom*. Alexandria, VA: Association for Supervision & Curriculum Development, 2014.

CHAPTER 3

Bender, William N. *Project-Based Learning: Differentiating Instruction for the 21st Century*. Thousand Oaks, CA: Corwin, 2012.
Headlee, Celeste. "10 Ways to Have a Better Conversation." TED Talk, May 2015. https://www.ted.com/talks/celeste_headlee_10_ways_to_have_a_better_conversation/.
———. *We Need to Talk: How to Have Conversations That Matter*. New York, NY: Harper Wave, 2017.
Morris, Lawrence D. *The Art of Conduction*. New York, NY: Karma, 2017.
Saphier, Jon, Mary Ann Haley-Speca, and Robert Gower. *The Skillful Teacher: Building Your Teaching Skills*. Acton, MA: Research for Better Teaching, 2008.

CHAPTER 4

Brown v. Board of Education of Topeka (1954). 347 US 483.

Emdin, Christopher. *For White Folks Who Teach in the Hood . . . and the Rest of Y'all Too: Reality Pedagogy and Urban Education*. Boston, MA: Beacon Press, 2016.

Government Accountability Office. *K-12 Education: Discipline Disparities for Black Students, Boys, and Students with Disabilities*. Report GAO-18-258 (2018). https://www.gao.gov/products/GAO-18-258.

Ladson-Billings, Gloria. *The Dreamkeepers: Successful Teachers of African American Children*. Hoboken, NJ: Jossey-Bass, 2009.

———. Keynote speech to Alliance for Catholic Education, University of Notre Dame, July 25, 2017. https://ace.nd.edu/news/dr-gloria-ladson-billings-addresses-ace-teachers-and-leaders.

Muhammad, Anthony. *Overcoming the Achievement Gap Trap: Liberating Mindsets to Effect Change*. Bloomington, IN: Solution Tree Press, 2015.

Stevenson, Howard C. *Promoting Racial Literacy in Schools: Differences That Make a Difference*. New York, NY: Teachers College Press, 2014.

Taylor, Elanor. "Groups and Oppression." *Hypatia* 31, no. 2 (2016): 520–36.

Williams, Joanna Lee. "'The Transformative Power of Diversity in Education Is Enormous': Challenges and Opportunities in the 21st Century." Child Development in a Diverse Majority Society Lecture Series, University of Virginia, July 2018. https://www.youtube.com/watch?v=RQF1K0AbkJY.

CHAPTER 6

Auer, Peter. *Code-Switching in Conversation*. New York, NY: Routledge, 1998.

Crenshaw, Kimberlé. *On Intersectionality: Essential Writings*. New York, NY: New Press, 2018.

Dweck, Carol S. *Mindset: The New Psychology of Success*. New York, NY: Random House, 2008.

Fosha, Diana. *The Transforming Power of Affect: A Model for Accelerated Change*. New York, NY: Basic Books, 2000.

Ginott, Haim G. *Teacher and Child: A Book for Parents and Teachers*. New York, NY: Scribner Paper Fiction, 1993.

Griffin, Joe, and Ivan Tyrrell. *Human Givens: The New Approach to Emotional Health and Clear Thinking*. East Sussex, UK: Human Givens, 2004.

Koppelman, Kent L. *Understanding Human Differences: Multicultural Education for a Diverse America*. London, UK: Pearson, 2013.

Lai, Calvin K., Kelly M. Hoffman, and Brian A. Nosek. "Reducing Implicit Prejudice." *Social and Personality Psychology Compass* 7, no. 5 (2013): 315–30.

Mehrabian, Albert. *Silent Messages: Implicit Communication of Emotions and Attitudes*. Belmont, CA: Wadsworth, 1980.

Shaver, Philip, Judith Schwartz, Donald Kirson, and Cary O'Connor. "Emotion Knowledge: Further Exploration of a Prototype Approach." *Journal of Personality and Social Psychology* 52, no. 6 (1987): 1061–86.

Spolin, Viola. *Theater Games for the Classroom: A Teacher's Handbook*. Chicago, IL: Northwestern University Press, 1986.

About the Author

Kristin Stuart Valdes is an artist and educator who began her work in New York City public schools as a teaching artist, in the disciplines of theater and creative writing, working with Henry Street Settlement and Teachers and Writers Collaborative. She began her work in the field of social and emotional learning while working with students who had witnessed 9/11 from their school building and who ended up calling one another "terrorists" in its aftermath. She has a deep interest in the roles that cultural practice, language, ethnicity, and class all play in the way we interact with one another, and in the way creativity contributes to our ability to resolve social and emotional problems effectively.

Valdes was the senior program manager of the 4Rs+MTP research study, funded by the US Department of Education, which delivered a social-emotional learning program and one-on-one coaching to teachers who delivered it, in over sixty public schools in the Bronx. She has worked with Morningside Center for Teaching Social Responsibility and the National School Climate Center as a senior staff developer and contributing writer. With Teachstone she has served as a mentor coach on a wide range of projects, including working with Native American teachers on Native American land.

Valdes is also an award-winning screenwriter and music-theater maker whose work has been recognized by the Academy of Motion Picture Arts and Sciences and presented at venues including Lincoln Center for the Performing Arts and the Brooklyn Academy of Music. She is a certified CLASS Observer and Trainer, is a Part 137 Mediator for New York City courts, and holds a BFA and MFA from NYU's Tisch School of the Arts.

Made in the USA
San Bernardino, CA
16 December 2019